THE
STRAWBERRY FAIR

Adventure, Danger, and a Surprise Gift

Shane Woods Series
Book Two

Dr. Tom Latham

DynoTech Publishing

Edited and published by Dave Carlson at DynoTech Publishing, Colorado Springs, Colorado, USA. (www.dynotech.com)

ISBN: 978-1-885708-52-6 (Paperback)

Library of Congress Control Number: 2026904685

First Printing: 2026

Contents

Captain Thomas Latham
Retired U.S. Army Chaplain

DEDICATION

I dedicate this book to my firstborn, Thomas William Latham. We must have taken 1,000 photos of him. He was born on September 11, 1969, in Owatonna, Minnesota, where we lived when we went to Pillsbury Baptist Bible College (PBBC).

Because we did not have a TV for our first three years of marriage, Penny spent many hours teaching Thomas Bible verses. By the time he was two years old, he knew many verses. At two and a half, he told me he wanted to accept Christ as his Savior. Since I never heard of someone that young getting saved, I tried to talk him out of it. He had a serious discussion with me about salvation and eternity, and convinced me he knew enough.

He was always respectful and obedient, trying to be a good example for his younger brother. Thomas was seven when we arrived in Brazil in 1976. He never took a class in Portuguese; he just learned it quickly by having to live in Brazil.

He was a model teenager, learning the guitar and reading his favorite magazine, *Soldier of Fortune*. He graduated from our home church's Christian school  and went to Army boot camp the next day. His drill sergeant told me, "Your son is not just a good soldier, he's also a very good Christian."

During his first year at PBBC, he served as the flag bearer in their parade. While serving at the school training foreign soldiers, he learned Spanish and was awarded the 'Soldier of the Year' for his installation.

Thomas served for two years in Korea as a married missionary. He had two children and served in Brazil for six years. During this missionary endeavor, he started 'Warriors of God' Jiu-Jitsu training for 100 kids.

He finished seminary and rejoined the Army as a chaplain, serving in Italy, Germany, Iraq, Afghanistan, and around the USA. He even received a medal from the Czech Republic for helping their soldiers. He is now Captain Thomas Latham, retired, and living here in Brazil.

The Latham family has always admired his patriotism and love for Christ and His people. I have the greatest admiration for him and his service to America and the Kingdom of God.

INTRODUCTION

Storytelling is one of my passions, and through my books, I strive to convey joy, encourage reflection on my faith, and move readers emotionally by sharing real-life experiences. If my stories move you emotionally, I have succeeded.

I am committed to presenting Christ as the only true Savior, and to showing that following Him wholeheartedly defines authentic Christian living. I also reveal the devastating impact the liquor industry had on my family, hoping to illustrate the destruction it can cause. It's a legal drug that sent my mother to prison and caused the death of my brother, Danny, at 49 years old.

Abandoned three times by my mother, I found refuge with my loving grandparents at their Crabtree Creek farm. Their care shaped my life. I have no idea where I would be today if it weren't for the tender care of my grandfather, John Taylor, and his wonderful wife, Julia.

Certainly, I wouldn't be where I am.

This book is written to inspire you to accept Christ as your Savior and commit fully to Him. My own journey began on May 6, 1964, when a fellow sailor, Richard Edwards, invited me to Calvary Baptist Church in San Francisco, California. During my Navy service, Richard and I shared our faith with others during sea voyages.

I spent ten years in formal Bible study. Our family arrived in Brazil on October 1, 1976. We started four churches, and I now pastor the fourth.

Some images and illustrations in this book were generated or enhanced using artificial intelligence (AI) technology to enrich your experience as a reader.

Dr. Tom Latham
Missionary and Wrestling Coach in Brazil

1 - Adult Runaway

Loretta Woods hurriedly packed what she could grab, heart pounding. She wrote a short note to the kids with shaking hands, tossed it in the freezer with the keys to the '51 Chevy convertible, and burst out the screen door, letting it slam as she ran down the road, desperate to disappear. Vini the Fin, the loan shark, wasn't going to grab her today—not today or any other day, she vowed, anxiety mingling with hope.

She had just gotten a surprise call from her childhood friend, Gloria. Gloria's voice shook as she warned, "Some unsavory characters are on their way to your house. The visit won't be pleasant. Get out and get out NOW. I'm not kidding, this is serious."

Loretta had been drinking and gambling—a combination often fatal for those for those with no self control or poker face. With no luck whatsoever, she now owed a large sum to unfriendly loan sharks, putting her and her children in danger.

Like many alcoholics, making wrong decisions daily is a lifestyle that brings sorrow, suffering, and even danger to those around them. Consumed by selfish fear and anxiety, she abandoned her children again, torn between guilt and a desperate hope that she was doing what was best for them.

This was the third time she abandoned her motherly obligations, knowing in her heart it was wrong, yet too many years lost to alcohol had eroded her ability to choose differently.

She clung to the hope that she would get back on her feet and reunite with the kids again, as she had done twice before. Right now, a heavy sadness mixed with relief as she told herself they were better off at their grandpa's farm in Oregon than with her. Each time, she made these heart-wrenching decisions without consulting them or her father, feeling isolated by her guilt and uncertainty.

Catching transportation at the bus stop in Hopland, she sat heavily in her seat, staring at her reflection in the window. A wave of regret washed over her as she thought of the few good days she had given the kids. There had been SOME days free from drinking—picnics, baseball, and swimming in the Russian River, which ran through Hopland and sometimes ran over it—memories tinged with longing and loss.

"Where to now?" weighed on her mind, anxiety churning in her stomach. She decided to head south toward San Francisco, feeling both uncertainty and a flicker of determination. The vastness of the city seemed to offer a chance to hide; clinging to this thought, she tried to calm her nerves, telling herself nobody could find her there.

San Francisco was buzzing with excitement as the Warriors basketball team, led by Wilt Chamberlain, was in the NBA playoffs. Maybe with all the extra tourist traffic, it would be easy for her to get a job as a waitress. She could sleep at the YWCA, as she had done so many times before, where no one would ask her any prying or embarrassing questions.

When the bus stopped in Santa Rosa, a big, blond man entered and sat in the empty seat next to her. He looked friendly enough, but Loretta was always suspicious, especially of men. He glanced her way and said with a kindly voice, "Are you going to San Francisco?"

She did not want to talk to anyone. Still, his demeanor was comforting, and she felt at ease in his presence. "I am and I'll be looking for a job when I get there." She did not know why she was giving this stranger her personal information. She was always cautious not to do so.

He inclined his head. "Do you have any idea where you'll search for employment?"

What did he think? Was he going to help her? Not many had ever helped her except her father, Jack Woods, and her long-lost high school friend, Gloria Dryer. She had discovered that she could depend on these two, although she rarely took their sage advice. If she had taken it more often, she would not be on this bus now, giving her personal information to a total stranger.

The stranger's voice stayed gentle. "Do you have family in the Bay Area? If not, where will you stay tonight?" His interest startled her; an uneasy flutter rose in her chest. No one outside her family ever showed such concern. Suspicion and anxiety mingled—no stranger asked such questions without ulterior motives. Her past experiences, after all, had led only to disaster for her and her children.

She struggled to decide whether she could trust this man, her apprehension rising. Was he really sent by the men looking for her? It seemed irrational, but her mind circled with doubt. Part of her wanted to believe he meant no harm, her intuition whispered trust, but years of fear left her conflicted.

"I plan to stay at the YWCA, where I've always been welcome." She realized she'd told him where to find her, but oddly, it didn't frighten her.

The tall blond smiled and remarked, "It's a lovely day that the Lord has made, isn't it?"

What is this, she pondered in her troubled heart? Was this another religious fanatic, someone about to confront her? Annoyance battled with exhaustion inside her chest. She was fed up with them—forever throwing Bible verses at her and insisting she keep THEIR set of rules. She felt a sense of resignation and even resentment, convinced these rules could never bring her peace or relieve her deepest problems of doubt and fear. This was her personal opinion.

That's it! She refused to continue the conversation. She didn't want an argument about the Bible or religion. She felt it was a waste of time and usually led to shouting. The one with the weaker defense always shouted loudest. That was always HER.

He nodded thoughtfully. "I also don't like to argue about religious things. We need more conversations about the goodness and kindness of God toward us. Don't you think so?"

"What's going on?" she wondered, discomfort prickling at her as if the stranger could read her mind. She felt conflicted by her desire to withdraw and the strange calmness she felt in his presence. Reluctantly, she admitted, "I haven't thought a lot about these subjects, especially lately," her voice betraying fatigue and confusion.

He leaned forward, refusing to be put off by her evasiveness. "What's happened lately that's made you uncomfortable talking about this?"

She finally had to put a stop to this; irritation and exhaustion blended. "I really don't want to talk about my personal life with a stranger." She hoped this blunt statement would grant her peace and signal her boundaries, though she felt its harshness linger.

But not this person. He was not offended and just kept on coming with his list of questions. "Where are you going to eat? Where will you find friends? Do you have any friends in San Francisco?" he pressed. He quickly noticed that if he continued his interrogation, she would move to another seat. So he retreated a little. "Okay, you don't want to talk, and I understand. I'll remain quiet the rest of the trip so that you can stay in your seat," he said quietly.

That suited her just fine; relief washed over her as she could now stare out the window, lost in thoughts of broken promises and abandoned children. Sadness and guilt pressed in on her as the stranger hummed a familiar church song, 'Wonderful Grace' or something like that—a tune she connected with funerals and solemn memories.

If it was grace, and grace meant 'freely given,' she knew nothing about this subject. If grace is freely given, it must be allotted to persons who deserve it, right? She knew in the depths of her heart she was not one of these persons. Nothing was 'FREELY GIVEN,' especially something as extraordinary as salvation. Why, it was only logical that it had to be earned, that it be sacrificed for. Then there was always the lingering fear that it was not enough. At least this is how she interpreted the religious stuff.

She had always told Gloria, "I believe in God, I think. Is there a judgment day? I doubt that there is. But if there is, God will give me just exactly what I deserve."

Gloria tried to explain it to her. "Listen, girl, mercy is God not giving us what we deserve—eternal punishment. And grace is God offering to us what we don't deserve—eternal life. For some odd reason, you believe God might be eternally kind to you because of all the things you've already suffered here. Am I seeing this right?"

Loretta had to be honest, "Yeah, that's about how I figure it's all going to play out. Show me where I'm going wrong, if you can."

"Friend, I've already shown you many times, but you still insist on clinging to your unbelief. Until you accept the Bible as God's only message to us, it's going to be impossible for anyone, including me, to convince you of your need to accept Christ. But honestly, don't you think most of your hard times have been the result of your own bad decisions?"

That is how the conversations usually went with Gloria. In Loretta's opinion, Gloria was close-minded and a pesky religious fanatic who was always trying to get her to see the errors of her ways and change, for the kid's sake, as she often said.

A pothole in the road jolted Loretta back to the present situation; another religious fanatic was sitting next to her NOW. Happily, in her favor, the trip would only last another half hour. Then she could get rid of the stranger who had taken such an interest in her personal life.

As they crossed the Golden Gate Bridge, she experienced a fleeting sense of relief, letting the setting sun's colors distract her. Yet the beauty felt distant and lonely—she had no one to share it with. She felt a pang of emptiness, unable to accept the idea of a creator or anyone watching over her.

At the terminal, the stranger stood and met her eyes with quiet compassion. "Loretta, I'm giving you a business card. Look up this man on the wharf. He'll be able to help you when you need it." With that, he strode off the bus, the first to exit. On the seat beside her, she noticed a fifty-dollar bill.

She was more concerned now. She had never given him her name. How did he know her name? Was this a reason for her to be alarmed? She hoped not. Now it was her turn to get off. She grabbed the fifty and stepped down; the stranger was nowhere to be found. Then she felt the cold, damp evening wind break across her face, so she pulled up her sweater hood. Welcome to San Francisco.

Loretta took a trolley to the wharf to look for a job. She was overwhelmed with the smell of lobsters and  clams as she worked her way through the eating galleries. The stainless steel tubs held the live, condemned sea creatures until someone chose them to be thrown into a pot of boiling water.

She talked to a few patrons about a waitress job but found no one interested enough, even to give her an application to fill out. This was not going to be as easy as she thought. She had to hurry to catch the last bus to get to the YWCA before they closed the doors for the night. She made it and crashed in one of their available bunk beds.

She did not immediately go to sleep. She was

an alcoholic and a gambler, but was not a mother completely devoid of feelings. She knew her decisions were causing her and the kids a lot of suffering, but she did not seem to see clearly enough to come up with other solutions. Escaping was always the easyist way out for her. Grandpa would take care of the kids again; he always did. He was a good man.

She wondered where the three of them were now. She had no way of knowing Thomas was on his way to San Diego to report for Navy boot camp and that Shane and Kosy were about to be incarcerated for the simple fact they could not prove the car was theirs. If she had known this, it definitely would have taken her longer to drop into la-la land. She did not exactly cry herself to sleep, as Kosy often did.

YWCA roll call was at 6:00 AM. She would get a continental breakfast and be ushered out onto the streets of San Francisco. She could come back for a bowl of soup at noon, and a place to sleep each night, but she had to spend her daylight hours on the city's dime. Therefore, she made her way back to the wharf, hoping that today she would be more fortunate in finding some employment.

Finding employment was getting to be a real trial, something she had never figured would happen. She usually could land a job within hours of starting to search. But not today—this was very strange for her to understand. After having no success and not wanting to return to the YMCA, she decided to take a look at the card the stranger had given her.

She fumbled around in her purse until she pulled it

out. It only had a man's name and address on it. In the bright afternoon sunlight, she squinted and read: "Dwyane Spear, 1098 Lumbard St."

She found The Crab Shack and asked for Dwyane Spear. The greeter went to the back and brought a kind-looking, older man to meet her. He wiped his sweaty hands on his already greasy apron and extended a friendly hand to Loretta. She eagerly accepted his warm reception.

Shoving the folded piece of paper towards him, she said a kind man on the bus gave her his business card. He took it with a surprised look on his face. "I don't have business cards, but this is my name and this is the right address." He was a bit taken aback, but was not a man to get his feathers ruffled easily.

Loretta found the whole ordeal with the man on the bus to be a bit strange, weird—something that gave one the goosebumps, for sure. But here she was, asking this man for a job. The best she could do was hope—hope, hope, hope—and trust that the situation was not hopeless.

Dwayne gave her a quick once-over and decided she needed a friend. She appeared to be a bit worn out, frazzled, maybe even at wits' end. He scratched his head and began slowly, "If you want a job, I need a waitress TODAY. Do you think you can help us? This extra traffic from the NBA finals is a bit too much for us to handle." He was hoping she would say "YES."

She did say yes with a lot of enthusiasm. "Wow," she pondered to herself. "The stranger really did help me out. I want to thank him, but didn't even catch his name. He knows my name, though, maybe he'll look me up. I hope so."

Dwayne was excited to get some extra help with the rush of hungry customers coming into his restaurant, The Crab Shack, at all times of the day and night. His clam chowder and sourdough bread were a favorite on the Wharf. When could she start? That was what he wanted to know right now. "Oh, by the way, what's your name?"

She hesitated briefly, then blurted out, "Olsen, my name is Linda Olsen." She wanted Loretta Woods to be as hard to find as possible. Maybe this would give her a chance to get her act together enough to retrieve her kids and get on with an everyday life, if that is what she decided she really wanted to do. Time would tell.

Not having any reason to think anything was wrong, Dwayne accepted her as a waitress on the spot. He handed her an apron and told her to wash up and start waiting on the customers; they would settle the other details later. This was just what Loretta (or Linda) wanted—a job, a full-time job. She just had to be careful to use her new name.

After the evening shift, Loretta was counting her tips. Wow, she had made good money on tips. This was going to be a good deal, her working at Fisherman's Wharf. All she needed was a little more to get herself an apartment to hide away. Dwayne was exhausted but content that The Crab Shack had done so well. He was also elated to have more help. This new girl, Linda, was going to work out well.

He stopped her as she was going out the door. "Where do you live, Linda? It's late, and I'll give you a ride home." He was trying to be as helpful as possible. She looked like she could use a friend and some help.

Loretta took a deep breath before answering, "I'm staying at the YMCA right now, just until I can get my feet on the ground and find an apartment to rent."

Dwayne liked her and wanted to help. "You don't have to stay there, we have a small efficiency on the second floor, that no one's using right now. You could stay here, and it would be more convenient for you. Is that okay with you?"

She was surprised another stranger would help her. It seemed as though someone else was pulling the strings of her puppet life. Was there really a God, and did He have some interest in what she was doing? It seemed like that, but she was not willing to concede anything except that Gloria Dryer was praying for her. That she knew for sure.

"I'll take your most kind offer, Mr. Spear." Then the janitor, Rocky Hartung, offered to give her a ride to the YMCA so she could pick up her bag. She accepted the offer with relief evident in her smiling face. At midnight, she was moved into her new living quarters, with a window view of the mighty Golden Gate Bridge. She felt like her luck was changing.

Before she dozed off that night, she spent a lot of time thinking about her children. Were they already at Grandpa's farm? Were they happier? She knew they would be safe there. Vini the Fin knew nothing about her family or their whereabouts. At least this is what she wanted to believe.

Loretta (or Linda), settled in for the long haul. She worked seven days a week to occupy her troubled mind, which was torn between being relieved for succeeding in finding a job and worrying about her children. Five weeks brought her almost $1,500 in tips. She planned to start looking for a place to rent so she could bring the kids to San Francisco. These were her last thoughts as she laid her head on the pillow and drifted off into la-la land.

The morning shift did not start until 10:00 AM, giving her a little time to take a shower and get more presentable. When she finally donned her apron and grabbed her order book, she almost fainted from fright. Her stomach jumped up into her throat. There coming through the door was Vini the Fin.

2 - Riding Lessons

It would be late June before Snow Peak lost all its winter coat. The calm waters of Crabtree Creek invited young, daring swimmers, while wiser Lacombites stayed out of the 'cold' water and waited for July or August. Foolhardy kids didn't care; they'd stay in the freezing rapids until their lips turned purple.

The county built the bridge across Crabtree Creek for logging. Its better days were past. Logging rights off Sleen Mountain had run out, along with the good fir and spruce. Neither the county nor the logging company maintained the old bridge. It stretched across the rapids, weather-beaten and aged.

The dust settled around Grandpa's farm now that logging trucks no longer passed just forty feet from the house. Grandma finally stopped yelling for the grandkids to stay off the dangerous road. Monday's wash could be hung in the sunlight without coming back dirtier than before.

Shane kept comparing his old home in the Golden State to his current surroundings. Northern California was called 'golden' because of its brown, burned-out grass on treeless hills.

August in Mendocino County was hot, at least 110 degrees. They could call him the California Sunshine Kid, but Shane preferred the Willamette Valley. Here, he could gaze on green hills all year.

The scent of evergreen lingered in the air, strongest after heavy rainstorms. Each winter, towering Snow Peak greeted him with its white cap. Shane's feelings for his grandfather's farm ran deep. "I feel at home here. I know this is where I belong. I love this place. I never want to leave."

"Yes, it's mean, dirty work living here in Linn County, but someone's got to do it," Kosy commented, "And I sure am glad it's us," referring to her soiled hands after picking strawberries all day.

Anyone could see the Woods kids' excitement about staying at Grandpa's. This farm was the only place they'd ever called 'home.'

They had been dragged from bar to bar and moved from town to town until they didn't know where they lived. Once, Kosy had asked her mother, "Where do we live, Mom?"

Loretta's answer was as blunt as her lifestyle. "Just tell people you live on four Firestones." She meant to sound clever, but it wasn't funny anymore. Life was grim; living in a house ruled by liquor was tormenting and soul-crushing.

"Four Styrofoams?" Kosy questioned innocently.

"NO, dummy! Four Firestones—they're the brand of tires on the car." This was a typical response the kids received from their calloused mother.

Thomas and Shane survived transitory life better than Kosy. The two boys had no deep feelings for their mother. They were numb from the treatment and saw it as a hardship to endure. Kosy felt differently.

Kosy resented being treated as a nuisance—just someone to be tolerated, getting in the way of a desired lifestyle. She carried profound scars, close to hatred.

Shane had tried to help Kosy, but each time he offered comfort, she rejected it, and her pain simmered into silent fury. Thomas managed to soothe her briefly in tense moments, reading the exasperation in her eyes, but never persuaded her their existence was less than a torment.

Shane hoped Kosy would accept Christ and forgive their mom. He was grieved by the distance between them. He expected their friends at the Rocking L ranch to help win Kosy over, giving him hope that things could change. That's one reason they spent so much time there—the other was the redhead living there. She was charming, fun, and spiritually years ahead of him, making Shane feel both admiration and insecurity.

The blue '51 Chevy crossed the old bridge carefully so it wouldn't rip a tire on the raised logs serving as guardrails on each side. Kosy was hardly awake as she ran a comb through her hair. "Do you really want riding lessons, or are you just trying to spend more time with Erin?" She had her doubts.

"Riding a horse has always been one of my goals," Shane promptly defended himself. "I certainly don't want to continue using a pillow between the saddle and me. It's embarrassing! You're right to a certain extent, though. I might not be quite as interested if the teacher wasn't so cute."

"Aha, so now we see the true motive for our new Lacomb cowboy," Kosy teased. "Well, I agree with you. Erin is really cute, but that means nothing to me. I like her a lot. She's kind and considerate. Just the type of person I've always wanted to have as a best friend. We've moved around so much I've never developed a best friend relationship with any girl."

As they pulled into the Lynch Ranch, Shane had a comment for Kosy. "I'm praying for you, Little Sister. You need to accept Christ as your Savior, too."

"I don't understand God," she answered bitterly. "He hasn't seemed interested in me. I know He exists; I see His creation everywhere. None of this happened by accident. But I'm not sure how I feel about Him. I haven't seen much concern for me."

Erin and Marty had already pulled out four horses, therefore Shane decided that was enough discussion for now. The fenced area was limited. Gravel roads and seldom-used hunting trails stretched out around the ranch. Many abandoned logging roads wound through the woods, waiting to be explored.

"Well, good morning to Lacomb's only two riding

instructors," Shane greeted the Lynches. "Do you have any pillows we can use, or are we just going to beat ourselves to death anyway?"

Erin pulled the horse's head down to slide the harness over its ears. "I'd like to hear about your talk with Pastor Ballentine, Shane." She was passively interested in this kid with such a personality, but unless he was 100% sold out to Christ, her interest would only be a passing one.

"Well, I do have something exciting to share with you. I finally got that problem resolved between God and me. I accepted Christ as my Savior. I suppose you two have been Christians for a long time."

Marty was glad to give his testimony to Shane. "Since our parents were Christians, we were always in church. It was easier for us to understand the truth. We were surrounded by it. I accepted Christ when I was two and a half, and by then I had already memorized 100 Bible verses. My dad tried to talk me out of it, saying I was too young to understand. But, I did understand perfectly.

"I knew I was a sinner, and I believed the Bible about where sinners go when they don't have Christ as their Savior. I convinced my dad I was ready to trust Christ. So, I did, and I remember the event as clear as if it were yesterday. Erin accepted Christ when she was four. Every day, I thank God for having Christian parents."

Erin was not going to be left out. "God has been very good to us, and we never want to forget it. Ingratitude is never appropriate. Especially when you think of all God has done to save us." She hoped Kosy was listening carefully.

Kosy was silent but fuming. "I've never seen how good God is. Is it even true? If God really loves me, I want proof." She was mature and hardened for eleven. Bad experiences often do that to kids; it just seems to go with the territory.

"Now, the first lesson for beginners," Marty mustered up his best teacher's voice, "is to always put the saddle on the horse's BACK with the horn pointing UP and to the FRONT."

"Now here's one Montana cowboy that's going to put The Three Stooges out of business," Shane laughed. "I don't claim to know much about horses, but that part is so obvious it doesn't really need to be explained, does it?"

Erin was trying to be serious. "Come on, Marty, get serious, or we'll never get these green horns broken in. To get on the horse, you put your left boot in the stirrup on the left side and throw your right leg over the saddle."

"In the syrup," Kosy exclaimed. "What do you mean, put your boot in the syrup?" (By this time, it was carnival hour.) Mr. Lynch was enjoying it all as he brought two more saddles from the barn.

"Now look what you went and done, Marty. Your stupidity is contagious. Kosy caught it, and now Shane will probably come down with it."

"Not me," Shane laughed. "I've been vaccinated against it. I eat smart pills every day." Shane showed them something in his hand.

"Those aren't smart pills, Shane," Marty insisted. "Why, they're nothing but sunflower seeds."

"Why look, Marty is getting smarter already." And with that, Shane popped the smart pills into his mouth.

Mr. Lynch decided to take charge before P. T. Barnum sent in the clowns. "I don't want Kosy riding Old Bucker. Shane will have to ride Old Smarty since we only have four horses today."

"Well, Old Smarty," Shane complained, "it looks like I'm in for an interesting day." With that, he patted the horse on the rump and tipped back his cowboy hat Marty had loaned him.

The foursome decided to have a cold drink before heading out. While sitting on the veranda sipping iced lemonade, Mr. Lynch caught Shane's attention. "I have something interesting you might like to see."

Shane and Kosy followed Mr. Lynch into the kitchen. The ranch-style house was new. Two sliding, glass doors led from the veranda to a wide hallway, where the walls were covered with Mrs. Lynch's needlework.

A plush Persian carpet stretched from one end of the house to the other. This was another proof that would convince any Christian the Lord had been good to the Lynches.

Mr. Lynch led them to his study at the end of the hall. His private room wasn't as well-organized as the rest of the house. Old-looking books were piled to the ceiling, and several stacks of newspapers decorated the room. Mrs. Lynch let him be the boss of this mess. He opened a closet and displayed his treasure.

"This is my coin collection."

There before them stood shelves of one-gallon jars filled with pennies. Shane was amazed. "What's this? Do you have your own copper mine?"

"Actually, I have saved all these pennies over forty years. When I was just ten years old, my Dad challenged me to save my pennies, and now I have over $8,000 worth here."

Kosy began calculating. "That would be over 800,000 pennies. Wow, they must weigh a ton! What are you going to do with them? Open a penny arcade?"

"Four thousand four hundred and nine pounds, to be exact. Well, I suppose I should take them to the bank so I can get interest for them. They're still here because I enjoy looking at forty years of consistent behavior. Does that sound silly to you guys?"

"Eight thousand dollars sounds great to me," Shane said. "Maybe we'll look at things differently when we get to be as OLD as you are, Mr. Lynch." Shane hoped he had not hurt his feelings.

"Old," Mr. Lynch slapped Shane on the back, "thanks for the compliment, Shane. You'll go a long way with that subtle attack."

Erin shouted from the veranda. "Come on, you guys, or we'll be late getting back for lunch. You can count Daddy's pennies later." She pulled the horse over to Kosy. "Mounting is not as easy as it looks. Do you remember what I said about getting aboard?"

Kosy put her left foot in the stirrup. "Mount on the left side, putting your tennis shoe in the syrup," she laughed as she swung her right leg over the horse.

Erin thought Kosy needed a little help, so she pushed her from behind. Kosy had already pulled on the saddle horn with all her might. With Erin's extra help, she slid off the right side and landed on the ground  with her hat flying west, and her loose hair covering her surprised face.

Shane had already mounted. "That's the shortest ride I've ever seen, Little Sister."

Kosy separated her hair with her hands and gave all three of them a good look at her tongue. "If Erin hadn't pushed me, I would've been high in the saddle by now." Erin felt sorry for what she had done, so she hurried to retrieve Kosy's fly-away hat.

Pulling out onto the gravel road, the four horses followed single file in one of the three ruts between mounds of gravel. "We have to leave two ruts for cars to pass," Erin insisted. "And hope they don't get friendly enough to honk."

Erin was not a novice rider. Ever since she could remember, she had owned a horse. She was from Belgrade, Montana, a small town located on the old Lewis and Clark Trail, only four hours' drive from the famous Yellowstone National Park.

The Lynches had lived in the shadow of Wyoming's Grand Tetons. Jim Bridger Mountain Ski Lodge and local rodeos were enough to keep teens busy. She really missed the Big Sky Country, but she was beginning to like it here. Lacomb, Oregon, had one thing Montana didn't—a handsome, blue-eyed, Christian boy named Shane.

She couldn't deny she was attracted to this California transplant, although he would have to be more than just a normal Christian, or her interest would stop there. Being completely sold out to God, willing to do anything He wanted, was the only kind of Christian life worth living. That was the way she felt about it, and she wasn't backing down for anyone.

Marty pulled off the road, pointing Old Bucker's nose up a well-beaten path. "Do you know where this trail leads, Shane?"

"We're now at the foot of Buzzard Butte. From afar, it looks like the back of a buzzard's head. This is an old logging road. It doesn't go very far up the mountain."

Caterpillar bulldozers dug out the old logging roads, which road graders continually smoothed. Usually, they were only wide enough for one truck to pass. When first built, they were laden with rocks. If they were not kept up or unused, the rocks washed away, leaving only the reddish brown dirt, hard-packed by the sun.

The trails were nice for riding. Marty said, "This particular trail has had a lot of trees fall on it. We'll have to be careful when we ride here."

When they cleared the trees, the horses began to trot. Shane and Kosy locked their knees, causing them to be thrown up about six inches and then roughly slammed back into the saddle.

Erin was amused by the sight, but felt pity for the rookies. "You greenhorns need to get a smooth rhythm. Flex your knees and move with the horse, or he'll beat your pants off," Erin insisted as she pulled alongside Shane.

"Keep your eyes open, Shane," Marty warned. "We didn't rename your horse Old Smarty for nothing." As they rounded a bend in the road, they came to a small meadow with knee-high grass. It contrasted with most of the area, thick with pine trees, which had no grass growing under them. The bases of these evergreen trees were blanketed with dead, brown needles, testaments to many undisturbed seasons.

Shane liked the calmness. He noted nothing but a slight breeze waving the maple trees and the sharp crack of a rifle. THE SHARP CRACK OF A RIFLE! Shane cocked his ear. "Is someone target practicing? There's no hunting in early June. Someone must be target practicing. But then again, why was there only one shot? That usually indicates poachers."

"POACHERS! I hate poaching," Marty barked. "Anyone who would poach is not only a lawbreaker, but he's a despicable character. My dad had better not catch anyone poaching around here. He'd run them right into the police station."

The rifle sounded again, suddenly shattering the taut silence they had been enjoying. Shane slowly, with calculated precision, turned his head from side to side. He was trying to get a bearing on the shots. Too quick and too few shots were the problem. He just couldn't zero in on the poacher.

Erin expressed her strong opposition to poaching, then suddenly changed the subject. "Kosy, do you like living here better than California? I'll bet you were always at the beach, and seeing movie stars, right?"

"I wish!" Kosy responded quickly. "We lived in northern California, one hundred miles from the beach. Even if you wanted to swim at Point Arena, the water was toooo cooold. As far as seeing movie stars, yeah, we did have a TV. And to answer your question, I love it here. At least I sleep in the same bed every night, and I know my grandparents love me."

This eleven-year-old had experienced too much of the world's wild side. She hated playing on the sidewalk outside the bar while her mom was drinking inside, and then having Thomas and Shane get Mom home—wherever home happened to be that particular week.

"That's really important for me, too," Erin agreed. "By the way, do you and Shane plan to take us to the Strawberry Fair?"

Shane started to smile inside when he heard his name mentioned. The good feeling soon worked its way to his innocent face. He was sporting a grin as wide as the desert horizon when he answered Erin. "That was my intention, Cowgirl. When do you want to go?"

She never invented adventures; that was for the more bold-hearted, and she had never been categorized as part of that exclusive group. "Well, I was hoping to have some fun and thrills. Do you suppose we can accomplish that without any trouble or adventures?"

"I'll do the best I can to accommodate you and Marty," Shane tried to assure her as he spurred his horse, leaping out in front of the rest.

Shane was serious about developing a relationship with this cowgirl. He kept tossing frequent backward glances at Erin as he pondered his situation. "I wonder if she likes me? I could come right out and ask her, but I couldn't chance another rejection right now. I'd better give it a little more time."

He was not paying attention to the trail in front, so he didn't notice Old Smarty had lowered his head. When Shane felt a pull on the reins, he turned around just in time to wrap his arms over a low-hanging branch. He had to hold on for life as Old Smarty just walked right out from under him.

As Erin caught up, she could not resist. "So, now what are you trying, a new form of dismounting? I think it has possibilities."

"No, I'm just hanging around, Cowgirl."

Kosy was about to make fun of her brother when a pair of scared Chinese pheasants fluttered in front of her horse. That spooked the mare, and she began a fast gallop. Kosy dropped the reins and held on to the saddle horn for all she was worth.

Chinese pheasants are very common in Linn County. The male is the one with the colorful head. There's a season for hunting them. Those who eat this bird say it tastes just like chicken.

3 - The First Encounter

When the horse wouldn't stop, Kosy grabbed the mane, then the neck, and bounced clear of the saddle. The untrained cowgirl wrapped her legs around the neck as she slipped off the side. "Help! Stop this thing!"

Shane was busy climbing down from a tree branch, leaving Marty to act. The sage horseman spurred his mount forward and grabbed the reins as he drew alongside. Kosy clung to two strips of mane, her tennis shoes dragging between the horse's front legs. Marty yanked the horse to a halt and watched Kosy slide limp to the ground.

Erin was the first to arrive at Kosy's side. "You all right, Kid?" Kosy answered with a protruded, exhausted tongue and an affirmative nod. Erin thought it would be all right to commence her teasing. "You and Shane sure do have innovative ways of dismounting! Maybe they'll become the new fad around Linn County."

Later that evening, as the sun set in glorious hues over what had been a hot, humid Oregon day, the migrant workers were fixing beans and frying pancakes to end their hard day's work, sitting outside the wooden shacks provided by the fruit-field owners.

The mosquitoes were resurrecting to begin their night of bloodletting.

It was a typical summer night in Lebanon—except it was STRAWBERRY FAIR TIME. Lebanon called itself the world's strawberry capital, with acres of plants stretching across Linn County. Berries are shipped nationwide. It was the town's only claim to fame.

Although Lebanon was a small town, it hosted a fair every year to celebrate its strawberry harvest. The town's people even chose a queen and planned a

parade, which gave all the youngsters a chance to ride through town on their favorite horse and provided the Veterans of Foreign Wars with one more opportunity to march proudly down Main Street.

This year, the fair was at the old high school football field. In 1960, the new school opened on 5th Street; the old high school became the junior high. Its front lawn—nearly two acres, shielded by tall firs—was too precious to use, so the fair took place on the empty field behind the school.

Old high school building in 1950. After the new high school was built, It became the junior high school.

The wooden football stadium was so old and weather-beaten it had to be torn down as a public safety hazard. Now, this area was used by the Santiam Elementary School for field events. Once a year it served as the fairgrounds. The Strawberry Fair was always scheduled during the first half of June.

The screams and laughter of kids and adults could be heard above the noise of the straining motors that ran the rides. The participants were forever complaining or exclaiming that their insides were now upside down on the octopus or rock-o-plane.

After the day's adventures, the '51 Chevy crossed Santiam River and passed Morse Lumber Company as the Lynches and Woods anticipated an evening of cotton candy and gravity-fed thrills.

Thomas was driving. He had only one week left of his leave before he had to report to San Diego for training in the elite Navy SEALS, the Underwater Demolition Team.

"Will there be any strawberry shortcake left for us?"

Marty asked, licking his lips.

"Of course, they've got tons of strawberries," Shane replied. "And there's an acre of shortcake, covered in mountains of whipped cream. Durham's Bakery makes it, and it's all free." He grinned. "My  taste buds are about to salute."

They pulled onto Tangent Street, considering themselves lucky to find a parking spot only three blocks away from the front gate.

Thomas locked the car. "You've got to be kidding," Shane said. "Anyone wanting in would just cut the canvas top." It was a daily worry for convertible owners, and Shane was one of them.

"Come on!" Kosy nudged Shane. "Rides first, shortcake after, as Erin wisely said." The group needed no further urging—they galloped toward the front gate.

Beside the entrance was a new attraction. "Step right up, kids," the well-dressed, smooth-talking announcer shouted. "See for yourself. The one and only, original armored car of Al Capone, the notorious Chicago gangster. It has six-inch, bullet-proof windows and a Tommy Gun in the back seat. Step right up ..."

"We'll have to catch that on the way out," Marty suggested as he headed straight for the rides.

"Hey, something else is new," Shane said, pointing down the row of games. "Clowns! Never seen clowns here before."

Three clowns wore so much makeup they were unrecognizable. They kept the crowd entertained by leapfrogging, doing headstands, and faking pickpocket acts. It was chaotic but amusing—an intense new attraction.

Carnival rides were thought up by people who ate worms and slugs when they were kids. One night, as an adult, they overindulged in garlic, woke up screaming—and pronto, a new nightmare ride was invented. These gut-twisters were developed with sadistic intentions. Who in their right mind would make such a scream machine? Who, with a lick of sense, would pay hard-earned money to have his body turned every which way but loose?

If one of those octopus cars ever broke away, passengers might find themselves flung right into the junior high swimming pool across the street. But the teens didn't mind; they were eager for adventure, ready to scream as they enjoyed the wild rides.

"Shane, got a penny?" Kosy called, stepping up to the penny-crushing machine. She could put one cent in and chose between *The Gettysburg Address* or *The Lord's Prayer*—she picked Lincoln's speech. She wasn't much on religious items; they had never seemed to help her when she was abandoned, crying herself to sleep at night.

The machine's workings were visible. The penny dropped, and the hydraulic press crushed it. Kosy could wear it as a necklace or keep it as a memento. Lincoln was her favorite president, known for his honesty.

"If we had my dad's penny collection to run through the machine," Erin said, "we'd be here until Shane was old enough to vote."

The happy-go-lucky clowns now surrounded the group and pretended to pick Shane's pocket. Shane was not entertained.

"All right, that's enough," Shane said. "You're good, but I'd rather keep my money—and my driver's license."

Suddenly, one of the clowns looked up, pointed to the sky, and grunted. As everyone was staring upward, another clown knelt on all fours behind Shane. Then, the first clown gazed right into Shane's eyes and pushed him backwards. It was an old trick, and Shane fell for it, literally. As he went flying backwards, the clowns ran off laughing, hoping to bring joy and happiness to some other hapless soul.

"Hey, those guys play a little rough, don't they,

Thomas?" Shane protested as he sat there on the hard-packed dirt, dusting off his used Levi's. This was not fun. "Something's off, and I want to get to the bottom of this."

Thomas helped his brother up, glaring after the clowns. "I'd chase them down—but let's not ruin our night. Still, why single us out? Maybe they don't like our faces."

The kids rushed to the stomach floppers. Each compartment on the rock-o-plane held only two people. Shane grabbed Erin's hand and shoved her into the oval-shaped torture room. "You're really going to like this one."

Erin voiced her opinion. "I have a feeling my stomach will end up in my throat—and that's not where I want it, Shane."

"I'll make sure it does," Shane shot back.

The lap bar could be adjusted to cause significant rocking or held in place to prevent any rocking. After the wire-mesh door was closed and locked with a pin, the motor roared, and the girls began screaming.

The Rock-O-Plane was not a ride for someone with motion sickness. Shane could stop the car at the top, or anywhere along the circular route, by pushing the lap bar forward. That would allow them the pleasure of standing motionless, their heads pointed 

downward, catching fleeting glimpses of the ground. When they were upside down, Shane heard all his loose change fall uncerimoniously to the ceiling.

"Shane, my hair's doomed," Erin moaned. "And I think I left my stomach on the last spin."

When the ride was finished, there was a mad race to recover the lost change.The operator hurried them out. "Move along. Others are waiting." As soon as they stepped back, he dashed for the coins. Shane helped Erin. "That was the priciest ride. I lost all my change— but at least not my supper. Time for strawberry shortcake."

The line to get strawberry shortcake was not long. Everyone got enough paper bowls to go up each arm. Even though Shane and Kosy had worked for weeks in the strawberry fields, they still enjoyed their dessert. There is something extraordinary about strawberry shortcake. It makes one's taste buds go into orbit.

Just as Shane was putting the first bite into his last bowl of summer delight, the painted menaces attacked again. One clown quickly swooped his hand under the paper bowl and filled Shane's face with strawberries and whipped cream. Another cruel clown promptly crowned Erin with the remains of her bowl.

That was the last straw! Thomas and Marty burst into action. They chased the clowns across the grounds as the crowd cheered them on. Everyone thought it was part of the act. Unfortunately, the Lacombites had stuffed themselves too much to make it to the front gate. The race was as short as the cake. Thomas and Marty collapsed on the midway as the painted plagues laughed their way out of the main entrance.

The rest of the '51 Chevy gang caught up just as Thomas and Marty were helping each other up from the turf. Erin was beside herself. "Look at what those creeps did to my hair." She asked Kosy to help her wash it out at the water faucet.

Marty was not going to miss a chance like this. "Well, friends, some days you are the bug and some days you are the windshield. It looks like this is your day to be the bug."

As the gang left the fairgrounds, Shane suggested they visit Al Capone's car. "We need to see how to defend ourselves from the Snow Peak robbers."

The grill from a 1925 Packard grinned menacingly at them as they stepped through the door. The front had a three-inch steel plate protecting the radiator. Thick, wavy windows made it hard to see 

inside. Two Tommy Guns were strapped to the back seat. The sliding window on the roof was used to ward off attacks from all sides. Steel plates decorated the wheels and protected them.

Thomas tapped the door. "You can bet there are steel plates in these doors, too. This car weighs 5,000 pounds and has a 200-horsepower motor."

Erin read the plaque.

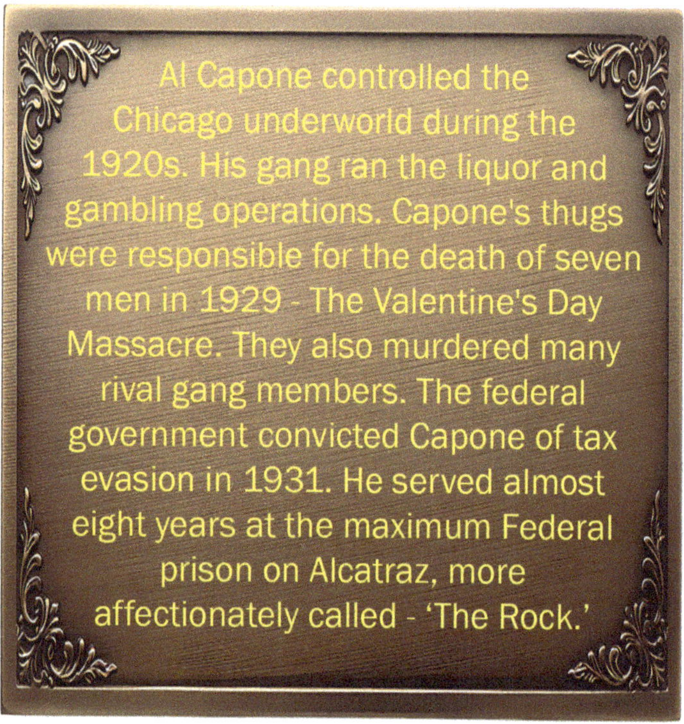

Marty looked shocked. "Can you imagine that. He did all those crimes, and the only thing they could get on him was tax evasion."

When Thomas walked out the gate, he turned to the guard to complain. "Those clowns you hired play a little rough. If they are supposed to bring joy and happiness to the crowd, they are obviously not accomplishing that."

"Those three clowns don't work for the fair," the guard replied. "I think the city hired them. But even so, I'll register your comment and pass it on to the fair officials. So far, you are the only ones to voice a complaint. Maybe they don't like you kids."

The Oregon night glowed with a full moon surrounded by glistening stars, like a king and his court. On brilliant nights like this, one could drive the country roads without using his headlights, but only fools would really do it. There was a slight breeze coming from the west, probably from the Coast Range. Although it wasn't enough to cool anyone off, it was just enough to keep the mosquitoes at bay.

As they strolled back to the car, passing under a street light, Marty noticed something. "Hey, Shane, take a gander at this white paint job. It looks terrible. I could do better with a roller."

"You're right, you could," Shane agreed as he took a closer look. "They must have painted it with a broom. Perhaps they are dirt poor, or were in a big hurry."

"Isn't this a '55 Chevy, four-door?" Thomas noticed as he passed his hand over the hood. Shane ran to the back of the Chevy. "Look, Kosy, some horse hairs are jammed into this cracked taillight.

"Shane, this gives me goose bumps," Kosy exclaimed as she began to trim her nails with her teeth. "You mean those three robbers are in the fairgrounds?"

"I'm afraid so, Little Sister," Shane agreed. "I think Marty and you guys should call Sergeant Kochian while I stay here and see which way the robbers might go."

"I'll stay with you, Shane," Erin offered. "We can hide behind those bushes over there." Erin was already reading her brother's mind, "Marty, we promise we won't mess with them. We'll only observe their actions."

"You knew what I was going to say," Marty complimented his sister. "Okay, on that basis, we'll round up Sergeant Kochian. But keep your word, Erin. If you get into trouble, I'll be more than just a little perturbed with you."

As the others raced to the car, Shane and Erin knelt between the bushes and the cyclone fence that surrounded the fairgrounds. When the '51 Chevy sped by, Shane crawled closer to Erin. She was a strange girl. This teenager certainly was brave and yet extremely attractive. He was so close to her now he could smell her Chanel No. 5.

Would he be able to impress this cowgirl? Or did he need to impress her? She was about as genuine as a person could be. What had really impressed him was her determination to serve Christ. Since he had accepted Christ himself, that seemed to be quite significant.

Could she ever bring herself to be interested in someone with a background like his? Her hair was so red it almost looked black in the shadows. He was so focused on Erin he did not see the three men approaching. Erin brought him back into reality by bumping her shoulder on his. "There they are, Shane," she whispered.

Shane returned to the job at hand. Three men were putting large handbags into the trunk. The tall man who opened the driver's door seemed to be the boss. His name was Horace Trader, and he was not a nice person, not someone to spend a holiday with. "Get in, Clem, before I get furious. I didn't like it at all dat we saw dose junior detectives again."

"You bet, Horace," Clem slammed the trunk. "Sometimes we hav' to make sure day get what day deserve."

"They saw us at the fair, Shane," Erin whispered in his ear. The other two were shorter and wore western-style jeans and jackets, with straw, cowboy hats that partially shaded their faces. It was too bad they had come out already. There was no way Shane and Erin could follow them, not unless they had some greyhound blood running in their veins.

Just as Horace was closing the driver's door, a garter snake about as thick as a broom handle slithered between Erin's knees.

Large Garter Snake

4 - Native American Friend

When God put enmity between the woman and the serpent, He definitely included Erin Lynch. She didn't just dislike snakes—she LOATHED them. Her most vivid and terrifying nightmare was being lowered into a pit of venomous, writhing snakes. Horrors! Given that, her reaction was entirely expected.

Erin let out a yelp and jumped to her feet, startled by the threat. Shane immediately stood up beside her, but could only gasp in shock. Both were clearly visible under the bright streetlight. Horace pointed at them and shouted, "Hey, look! It's dose nosy kids again! Let's show dem a lesson once and for all."

At Horace's threat, Shane and Erin quickly turned and ran. With no other options, they headed straight into the carnival parking area. The fair crew kept their living quarters there in old, worn, semi-trucks and trailers. Since some crew members used live animals in their acts, animal cages were kept between the trucks.

Shane dragged Erin while his heart pounded. "We have to hide. We can't outrun them. Where are those clowns when you need them? They'd teach these guys a lesson."

Scanning desperately, Erin spotted a trailer with wooden walls extending from the bed to the ground. One wooden wall had a round hole, about the size of a large beach ball, just big enough for a person to fit through. She dove toward the hole, motioning frantically for Shane to follow. "Follow me, Shane! They won't see us in here," she whispered urgently.

Shane scrambled after Erin, hearing Horace's angry shouting grow louder as he approached. The two managed to hide under the trailer just before the bad guys ran past, not noticing them. A moment later, the pursuers returned and stopped directly in front of the hole.

Horace shined his weak flashlight on the opening. "Day certainly wouldn't crawl under dat trailer. We lost dem again. Rats, we almost had dose two kids in our hans."

With the criminals gone, Shane and Erin stayed hidden, puzzled by the thieves' certainty they would not be under the trailer. As the adrenaline faded, both noticed an unpleasant smell and wrinkled their noses in discomfort.

"I certainly hope this is mud we're kneeling in," Erin pleaded. She didn't like to get dirty, especially her hair. She was a real princess waiting for a wonderful prince to find her.

"Let's escape before we suffocate," Shane urged, sliding out ahead of Erin. Once free, they read the

sign on the semi-trailer: 'ELEPHANTS - LIVE CARGO.' When the others arrived with Sergeant Kochian, Shane and Erin were scrubbing the smelly elephant manure from every exposed patch of skin.

Marty was angry. "I thought you were just going to observe, Erin. And, what's that terrible smell?" He had a mischievous grin on his face as he realized what had happened. "Maybe if you wiped your hands and legs with stink weed, it would help."

"Oh, be quiet before I rub my hands in your face," Erin said disgustedly. She hated anything that took away her every-day, lady-like appearance away.

"Stink Weed"

Shane addressed Sergeant Kochian without even trying to shake his hand. "It was the Snow Peak robbers again. We think they must've been at the fair, because we heard them say they had seen us. They hightailed it west again. Sorry, we lost them. I suppose we haven't really helped too much, have we?"

The burly sheriff unclipped his radio. The streetlight glinted off his badge. He prided himself on keeping the community safe. "I'll put out an APB on them."

"What's an APB?" Kosy wanted to know as she kept her distance from the hapless teens, wrinkling her nose at the two unfortunate elephant lovers.

Marty was glad to inform her. "An APB is police talk for 'ALL Points Bulletin.' It means they're telling everyone to keep a lookout for the robbers."

"Oh, by the way," Shane added, "They painted their car white, and the new license is JOV 567."

Sergeant Kochian was taking down notes. "Now that you know their car, they'll probably dump it and steal another one. You kids are always around where the action is. Do you read Dick Tracy a lot?"

Thomas pinched his nose as he edged over to Shane. "Be sure and get all that fertilizer off before you get into our car."

"OUR car," Shane responded, shocked. "I thought it was MY car. You haven't changed your plans, have you, Big Brother?"

"I guess you're right," Thomas corrected himself. "Let's get home. But on the way, we have to stop and get gas."

On the way out of Lebanon, the blue Chevy pulled into a Texaco station. A large young man wearing a Stetson western hat came out to attend to them. He wore cowboy boots and appeared a bit bowlegged.

Since Shane was driving, he got out to meet the attendant. "Two bucks worth of regular, and you can change the air in all four tires. We've had that old air in those tires for over a year. About time for a change, don't you think, partner?"

The big guy responded, "That's really cute, it must be a new one. At least I've never heard it before. And I thought I'd heard 'em all."

Shane noticed this kid was massive and stocky. Shane only came up to his shoulder. His olive brown skin made his straight hair look blacker than midnight. "We were noticing the name of your station. What does the T.P. stand for?"

"That's my dad's initials, Travis Pinetree."

Shane was getting really bold now. "Are you by any chance of Native American descent?"

"That's right, Friend," he answered as he rounded the pump off to two dollars. "We're full-blooded Nez Pierce."

As Shane was paying for the gas, he noticed a warm, friendly smile spreading across the boy's face. Shane felt he could really like this kid, even if the big guy did outweigh him by at least one hundred pounds. "I presume you'll be attending high school here?"

"Yes, I'll be a freshman at Lebanon High." The Nez Perce had not seen customers quite so talkative or interested in what HE was doing. This might prove to be an exciting contact.

"Good grief, he's got six more years to grow," Shane

thought. "If he's this big now, he'll be bigger than a horse by the time he gets out of high school."

"Shane, can you hurry up?" Erin pleaded from the car. "Can't you chat tomorrow? I have to get home and get this ... this yucky stuff off my body."

"By the way, my name is Bowie, Pinetree of course," he said as he held out his hand. "What's your handle?" Unfortunately, they shook hands.

"Shane, Shane Woods, and just for your information, my grandfather was a full-blooded Cherokee from out around Ohio way. Can we talk again?"

"Sure, I'm here every day from 4:00 PM to midnight."

"Shane, please," Erin begged.

Shane advanced towards the car. "Got to go, see you soon, Bowie."

Bowie was sniffing his hand. "By the way, Shane, what is this terrible smell?"

Later, as the car pulled into Lacomb, everyone was complaining about the airs that Shane and Erin were putting on. "Poor Erin," Shane thought, "such a prissy girl and all covered with ..."

"Just for your information, fellows," Shane informed them, "that's the last time I'm following a girl under a semi-truck trailer. Mark it down."

Erin was defensive. "At least we did get away, didn't we, Shane. Don't be too critical, now. What was your plan to save us, disappear?"

Thomas was also feeling just a little bit sorry for Erin. "What do you say we go to the fair on the last night? I hear they're giving free elephant rides."

"Great idea," Marty added with a chuckle. "It's better to be on an elephant's back than under its trailer."

"Let me out of this car," Erin demanded as they pulled into the Rocking L Ranch. With that, she bolted through the door and made a beeline for the bathroom.

Marty was waving goodbye to the Woods. "Wait a minute, Shane. If you come over tomorrow afternoon, I'll give you your first wrestling lesson. Don't eat anything three hours before."

Shane looked surprised. "Is that a threat or one of the dark secrets of the wrestling world?"

"Well, if you eat anything before you wrestle, you might eat it again. Do you follow my point?"

"I'll take your word for it!"

On the way home, Thomas questioned Shane. "I've

been meaning to talk to you. What's happening around here? First, Grandpa and Grandma start going to the Baptist Church. Then they quit smoking and drinking. Now you also start getting religious on Kosy and me."

"Getting religious is not exactly what happened to me," Shane responded defensively. "Anyone can be religious. Remember, we all were baptized as babies in a church in Scio? That's religion; a decision made for me by others to get me closer to God.

"What I really needed was to recognize I was a sinner, repent of my sin, and accept Christ as my personal Savior. And I did. Christ is the way to heaven. Salvation is in a Person, Thomas, not in a process or a church. That's exactly what you and Kosy need to do—accept Christ. I'm praying for both of you."

Thomas didn't mind that. "Thanks, Brother, I can use all the prayer I can get."

Shane was very serious. "Perhaps you'll get an opportunity to talk to Pastor Ballentine before you have to leave. He's really a nice guy. He was a gunnery sergeant alongside Patton when the general walked all over Europe."

The next afternoon, refreshed after the previous night's events, the Woods kids drove to the Lynch Ranch. They went the long way around to show Kosy the Green Mountain Elementary School, where she would begin classes in a few months. Both Thomas and Shane had attended the school when they were juniors. It was the same two-room schoolhouse their mother had attended 30 years ago.

Shane even told them what he remembered. "Many times we had to walk the three miles to school. Usually, we met the neighbors and walked with them. We had to walk home, too, unless it rained. Then a kind neighbor would come and give us a ride."

"The two-room country school is fading into history," Thomas told Kosy. In fact, this will be Green Mountain's last year. It will be quite a switch from the other schools you have attended. Mom and her brothers even went here. At least now the plumbing is located inside."

Kosy stiffened at the mention of her mother. Now was her opportunity to talk to Thomas about her unanswered questions. She looked as serious as she could. "Thomas, now that you mentioned our mother, maybe you can give me some answers that Shane can't."

Thomas was always ready to help his sister, whom he loved so much. "Shoot, Kosy, I'm ready to field questions!"

Kosy continued. "Shane has been talking a lot about religion lately. I mean accepting Christ, of course. What I don't understand is how God could say He loves us when He allowed us to be mistreated by our mother. Can you explain that? Does God really love us? If so, how can we know?"

Thomas did not have the answers Kosy needed. "Before, I tried to explain how mom loved us, even though she treated us like she did. I don't think I ever convinced you, did I?"

Kosy shook her head with a smirk and a firm negative answer. Her question was the subject of stacks of books by different authors seeking the answer, many of them using the Old Testament figure of Job as a reference.

But Thomas had not read any of those books, and he certainly was not familiar with the story of Job. This young sailor was searching his untrained mind, trying to give his sister a suitable response. He was really struggling. "Now you have thrown God into the problem. I really can't answer you, my little sister. But I'd venture to say Pastor Ballentine could. Why don't you go and talk to him?"

No one had the answers she so desperately needed, but they all kept telling her the same thing: "Go talk to Pastor Ballentine." She wanted to ease Thomas's mind. "Maybe I will, Brother. Maybe I will."

Shane continued his interrupted tour guide session. "Next year, Green Mountain will be consolidating with

Lacomb's elementary school. This year, you'll have the same teacher they had last year, Mr. Gene Young. He's a nice man, about six feet seven, and reeeeal skinny."

"But watch out, Kosy. Don't get into trouble," Thomas warned. "He has a shoe size seventeen, and it can really make a nice impression on your backside."

"I was so young when I went to the first grade here, but I do remember a few things. Wasn't my teacher Mrs. Irene Larson? And didn't they use a big pot-bellied stove to heat the room? Are you sure I'll like it now?"

"Yes, yes, and YES, you'll like it," Shane assured her.

"Every cold-winter Friday, the kids bring vegetables and put them in a large pot. By lunch time, the stew is ready. Now, let's scoot on down to Erin's place." Erin lived at the foot of Gentry's Hill, where five roads met.

From Gentry's Hill to Five Corners, there exists a very sharp decline. Thomas was on a safety campaign. "On gravel roads, you have to be very careful, Shane. You can't stop on a dime and get nine cents change. If you brake suddenly, the road turns into a million tiny marbles. There's no way to control where you'll go, and when you'll stop."

Shane pulled the nose of the '51 Chevy over the rise and shifted into neutral. "Trying to save gas, Shane?" Thomas asked. "I hope you have good brakes!"

By the time Shane was halfway down the hill, he was topping forty-five miles per hour. It was time to start braking. A slight pump on the brake pedal, and Shane's eyes went wide open. The pedal slammed all the way down to the floorboard. He tried to shift into first gear but only ground the gears, so he stopped, lest he destroy the transmission.

"Great Scott," Shane yelled, "we have no brakes!" He started sweating profusely, and his adrenaline peaked. There was a logging truck entering the crossing at the bottom of the hill. If everyone didn't pay attention, there would be a terrific accident at the crossroads.

"God help us," Shane prayed.

Kosy hardly had time to start munching on her fingernails!

5 - The First Wrestling Lesson

Shane blew the horn, warning the truck driver to speed up and clear the crossing. The trucker noticed, floored the diesel, and ominous clouds of black smoke poured from both exhaust pipes.

Shane tried forcing the transmission into second gear. His desperate effort produced only harsh grinding noises. Unfortunately, this teenager's car never had an emergency brake. Why should it? Teens never expect emergencies, and if one happens, they think they can handle anything.

Kosy was wide-eyed and having a snack with her fingernails. The best Thomas could do was to cross his fingers. That is about the best any non-Christian can do.

Shane was different. Now that he had Christ as his Rock, he could pray for help. "Lord, send us help, now!"

Shane hit fifty-five as the car sped toward the crossing. The truck cleared most of the crossing, except for one long log stretching into Shane's lane. They ducked, and the Chevy passed underneath as Shane kept steering.

The Douglas Fir hung just low enough to tear off the canvas top. Instantly, 'Bluebird' became a homemade convertible. The worst was over, leaving just the challenge of keeping the Chevy steady until it stopped.

When they finally quit rolling, Shane was the first to speak. "Thank God that truck driver was paying attention. That's the fastest answer to prayer I've had."

The driver checked on them, found they were fine, and left. "Thanks for your concern. We're all okay, just feeling like a peeled banana," Shane said, eyeing the ruined canvas top, with pieces scattered all over the road.

A quiet group arrived at the Lynch ranch. Kosy immediately explained why the car had no top. Pulling her hair on both sides, she said, "It was another one of Shane's scream trips."

Mr. Lynch crawled under the car and looked at the brake line, coming up with fluid all over his hands. "It just simply wore through, Shane. I think Thomas and I can fix it if you and Marty want to work out. Go ahead, get going, Marty's already warming up in the wrestling room."

After thanking Mr. Lynch, Shane left the garage and headed toward the wrestling room, his mind buzzing with curiosity about what was to come. This could be very interesting. Even though he knew it was fake, he had always liked watching the Saturday night wrestling on TV. But Marty had already informed him this was entirely a different matter. Whatever that meant, he was about to find out.

Marty was stretching out his leg muscles. Shane entered and filled him in on the latest adventure. Marty just smiled as he shook his head. "You probably learned what a quick prayer is like, didn't you?"

"Yeah!" Shane responded. "And Kosy's fingernails didn't help; neither did Thomas crossing his fingers. I'm glad I have more to depend on. Now, are you practicing for a rubber man act at the fair?"

"It's very important to loosen all your body parts. Do what I do so you won't pull a muscle. Sit-ups, push-ups, pull-ups, and all other 'ups' help loosen stiff, unused muscles so they wouldn't tear and get you a bench-warming job for half the season."

"Did you hear the Giants' game last night?" Shane asked as he mimicked every move Marty made. "Willie Mays hit his 15th homer, and this is only June. How is Mantle doing?"

"Mantle's right up there," Marty defended. "Looks like the Yankees will be in the Series again if Whitey Ford holds up. Let's listen together."

Having loosened everything in preparation for their workout, Marty tossed Shane a pair of wrestling shoes. His aim was off, causing the shoes to wrap around Shane's neck. Both boys doubled over with laughter.

Marty smiled. "Nice necklace! I promised you the shoes if you practiced. They're your size. Make sure they're snug—after you get them off your neck!"

"The priorities of wrestling, in order, are: conditioning, balance, speed, moves, strength, and desire."

Shane frowned. "Isn't strength the most important? It looks like that on TV. Why do you say it isn't?"

"You need to forget TV wrestling," Marty said. "Strength matters, but it isn't everything. Did I show you my weight room?"

Shane peeked inside. "Wow, you've got everything. If strength isn't a top priority, why lift all these weights?"

"Because, if in all other areas you are equal with your wrestling opponent, desire and strength are the only variables left. Although strength is almost the least important, it CAN win you some matches."

"Do you think I can succeed? I know nothing about this sport," Shane admitted.

"If you wrestle all summer and don't like it, you can stop, no criticism from me. I think you have great potential," Marty encouraged.

"How can you say that? You haven't even seen me wrestle."

"True," Marty replied. "I'm judging your personality, not your ability. I think you can do well at anything you try."

Shane was humbled. "You really know how to make a guy feel good. Do I have a shot at varsity?"

"Probably not the first year. Few freshmen do. Coach Hazewinkle will let you try for varsity, but you'll need to beat a guy six feet tall. How's that sound?"

"You can't be referring to that big Native American at the gas station. What was his name, Bowie Pinetree? He outweighs me by almost one hundred pounds?"

Marty struggled with one of the dumbbells. "Get serious, Shane. That big guy would only have to sit on your chest to make a pancake out of you. The kid I'm referring to weighs a little more than you."

"You have to be kidding. Someone who weighs the same as I do is six feet tall? He would be so skinny his muscles would look like mosquito bites on spaghetti."

Marty continued, "The Lebanon Warriors have a junior varsity wrestling team. That's where the freshmen participate. It'll give you a lot of experience on your own level."

Shane was grunting on the bench press with a 150-pound barbell just above his chest. "Help me,

Marty." When he was relieved, the subject continued. "What about this coach guy Hazelrinkle? What kind of person is he?"

"It's HAZEWINKLE," Marty corrected him. "He's excellent. Jim used to coach the West Point wrestling team. He's won the AAU national championship ten times and has been on two Olympic Greco-Roman teams. He really knows the moves and is a fine Christian, too."

With their conversation about Coach Hazewinkle finished, Marty clapped his hands. "Now let's learn some basics, and afterwards we can pump some more iron, okay, Shane?"

"Sure, boss, whatever you say."

Marty moved to the center of the mat. "Legs about eighteen inches apart, knees bent, arms extended with palms open, and your shoulders in front of your knees. Your head must always be erect. Always look your opponent right in the eyes."

"Now pay attention." Marty made a lightning-quick move that threw Shane to the mat. The surprised victim was flat on his back, making it easy to get a good look at the ceiling.

As Shane allowed Marty to help him up, he stuttered,

"What ... what happened?"

"That was a single-leg takedown and a cradle hold for a pin. Did you get the ceiling tile counted?"

"What am I doing here? I feel like I did the first time my cousin Larry checkmated me in just three moves. Awful! But I eventually learned how to checkmate, too, so watch it next time, Pilgrim. Seriously, will I ever learn to do that?"

Marty felt just a bit ashamed of himself. "Sorry, Shane, I was only showing off. Sure, you'll get good, probably better than me. Now here's the single-leg takedown in slow motion."

Shane turned out to be a natural. After just fifteen tries, he could use the move, though Marty wasn't putting up much resistance. Still, Marty sensed potential for a champion if Shane applied himself.

"I'm amazed at how fast you catch on. Are you sure you've never had any wrestling experience?"

"None whatsoever, unless you count 'wrastling' with my brother, Thomas, when we were fortunate enough to have some grass to fall on."

Marty was impressed. "Shane, what you need is one good takedown and a few moves to confuse the opponents. If you use just one takedown, you'll be marked for that, so you vary your moves. Like the Giant's pitcher, Juan Marichal. He has three different angles he pitches the same ball from."

The twosome practiced the single-leg takedown for an hour, stopping periodically for Shane to catch his breath. "This is harder than hauling hay in Hopland, California, at high noon. And some of those alfalfa bales weighed even more than I did."

"A match is divided into three two-minute periods. The first period begins with both wrestlers starting in the neutral position. That means they are standing and facing each other. The other two periods start with the wrestlers in the referee's position."

"Most wrestlers are trained to set up on their opponent's left side for the referee's position. We're going to practice setting up on the right side. That'll really confuse most wrestlers."

Shane paused to rest. "May I be so ignorant as to ask why setting up on the right side will confuse the other wrestler?"

"They've practiced all their escapes as their opponent was latched onto their left side. Setting up on their right side will throw all their escapes into confusion. Any small advantage is worth working for."

Afterwards, Marty was doing curls with the barbells. "I'm sure glad you became a Christian, Shane. We've been praying for you since we got here and met your grandparents. They sure are wonderful people."

"I owe them more than I could ever repay," Shane got really serious. "They've taken us in three times and always loved us like their own children. I'm sure glad they're Christians. They're responsible for my salvation. Now we have to pray for Thomas and Kosy."

"That's good, Shane," Marty agreed. "But what'll really make a difference to them is to see a change in your life, a sincere desire to follow Christ. That will speak volumes. There are enough 'religious' people in the world; we don't need any more of them confusing the general population. What we need are followers of Christ who put Him first and live the life He wants. This'll attract the non-believer's attention. God wants total custody of His children, not just weekend visits."

"I really don't know much about the Christian life," Shane responded. "But, like wrestling, I'm willing to learn. What you say must be true. The first thing that got me thinking about Christ was the significant change I noticed in my grandfather's life. He pounded it into me that Christ made the difference, not religion.

"Unfortunately, Kosy hasn't gotten the point yet. She's so bitter against Mom she can't see how God loves us. Frankly, I can't answer her hard questions, yet. Maybe Pastor Ballentine will be able to."

The experienced wrestler nodded his head in agreement. "That's a question that preachers

have always had a hard time explaining. Jeremiah was a man of God, but was thrown into a muddy well. I'll pray for her even as I have for you. Shane, if you live the Christian life like you wrestle, then God will have all He wants of you. I believe that's what will make a difference to Thomas and Kosy."

Marty looked a little sheepish but was dying to know, "Excuse the question, I don't want to embarrass you or anything like that, but how is it that you are fifteen and only a freshman? Usually, kids who are fifteen are at least in their sophomore year. Just asking, if you don't want to answer this question, you don't have to."

"My wrestling teacher," Shane put his hand on his hips, "I do not take offense. First, I missed the cutoff date by 3 days because of my birthday. And secondly, we moved so much that I didn't get enough days in the first grade, so they held me back. Thomas always told people it was because I didn't learn my colors. Do you have any other questions you want to ask while I'm still in the mood to answer them?"

Erin peeked her head into the weight room. "Okay, Charles and Stanley Atlas, supper is on the picnic table. Come on, if you're hungry?"

"We can either shower after supper or jump in the creek behind our house," Marty

Charles Atlas
1950s Bodybuilder

proposed to Shane as they sat down to fried rainbow trout and lettuce salad.

"I like the creek idea," Shane answered as he passed the potato chips to Kosy. "Have you ever swum at the covered bridge? There is a nice flat rock and a rope to swing out over the water. Let's go there tomorrow evening, and then we can also visit Roaring River Fish Hatchery. They have a few humongous sturgeons."

Mrs. Lynch motioned for the girls to start clearing off the picnic table. "What's this story about going to the Strawberry Fair again, Shane?"

Before Shane could muster up a word for himself, Kosy decided to answer for him. "We go a couple of times every year, Mrs. Lynch. Every year we've been here, anyway. There are lots of rides. Don't worry, we're not going to gamble away our money on those foolish games. Our grandparents wouldn't let us anyway."

"We need to contact Bowie Pinetree and see if he's interested in going to the fair with us," Shane suggested, heading for the phone. "Can I use your phone, Mrs. Lynch?"

Mrs. Lynch answered affirmatively. "It's a party line, like yours, so check to see if anyone is using it BEFORE you start dialing."

Many people in this area of Oregon couldn't afford private lines, so they were put on a party line with three to five other families. Each family had its own particular ring. Maybe a short and two longs or three shorts. The family's ears got trained to respond to their special ring.

Party-Line Phone System

If someone was conversing and a neighbor picked up the phone, they would hear a distinctive 'click.' The distinctive click made it possible to know if someone was eavesdropping. If both parties picked up the receiver at the same time, there was no way for either to know someone else was listening.

For anyone who was crude enough to do it, a party line was a great means of learning the latest gossip. Lacombites were very careful about what they said on a party line phone! No one wanted everyone to know all the family secrets.

"Hello, Bowie, Shane here. Would you like to go to the Strawberry Fair with us on Saturday evening? It's the last night. Sure, you can meet us at the archery range. We'll drop you off at home afterwards."

Erin was in her bedroom with her newest best friend. "Kosy, what's your brother like? I really haven't had a chance to talk seriously with him."

"Both of my brothers are very kind. They looked after

me all my life, even feeding me and changing my diapers," Kosy said with a blush. "My mother never cared for any of us. We were left to fend for ourselves. We never knew who our dads were. They left us when we were all young. We knew what every bar in Linn County looked like. I know others have had it worse than I have, but that never made me feel any better."

Erin looked very sympathetic. She could sense the bitterness in Kosy's young voice. She put her arm around the Woods girl. Here was a friend who needed to know the love of God. "I can't even imagine how that would be, Kosy. I've always had such good, faithful, Christian parents."

Kosy continued. "Shane has dedicated himself to taking care of me. Now he even prays that I'll be saved. I've got to get up to the parsonage sometime and talk to Pastor Ballentine. He seems to be the only one who might be able to answer my questions about the love of God."

Erin already knew about Kosy's problem and didn't feel qualified to answer her, so she changed the subject. "Does Shane have a girlfriend in California? You know, someone he writes to?"

"There were a lot of girls chasing Shane because he is so good-looking." Kosy snickered. "But, he had so many responsibilities with me he didn't pay much attention to them. Besides, they were mostly a bunch of knuckleheads."

Erin was delighted to hear that. She continued the Sherlock investigation as she started to twirl her fiery red hair with her index finger. "Is Shane interested in girls ... ah, what I mean is ... ah, well, what I'm trying to say is ah ... would he date a girl now?"

Kosy was getting humored by Erin's obvious bashfulness. "Why don't you ask him yourself? He'd probably be glad to tell you."

"Maybe I will, Kosy. Maybe I will," whispered Erin, as she walked away.

In 2014, I visited Roaring River Fish Hatchery with two of my grandchildren. Notice the huge rainbow trout in the holding pond.

6 - Roaring River Poacher

Larwood Covered Bridge on Crabtree Creek, a historical site, was a place for wonderful family times—swimming, swinging on the rope, splashing, and startling rainbow trout.

"Are you sure you remember the way to the covered bridge, Shane?" Grandpa asked as he picked up his welding mask. Jack Woods was a busy hobby farmer, constantly juggling tasks, but his devotion to family came first.

"Sure, Grandpa, just keep turning right and we'll

find it—and the fish hatchery, too?" Shane replied confidently.

"As right as rain. Now off you go." Jack cared deeply for his grandchildren. This was the third time he had taken them in. He always sought to guide his daughter, Loretta, down a better path—even if she resisted.

As they arrived at Rocking L Ranch, Erin shouted, "Kosy, your epidermis is showing!"

Kosette glanced all around her and began patting her arms and legs in confusion. "Where, where is it showing? I don't see anything."

Shane informed her. "It's just a trick, Kosy—you fell for it. You'll need a lot of practice to keep up with the Lynch kids."

Thomas came to everyone's rescue. "Let's make like a tree and leave."

The covered bridge, a rare historic structure, still stands at Crabtree Creek and Roaring River after 100 years, serving its purpose despite a few creaks and groans.

Covered bridges feel special—earthy history before your eyes. The old planks creaked under Shane's wheels as he crossed.

Thomas used his tour-guide voice. "Why are some bridges covered?"

"To keep the planks from rotting," Erin said.

"To keep snow off," Marty guessed.

"Nope," Thomas teased, "If so, why are there covered bridges in the South where it never snows?"

Kosy laughed. "Okay, Thomas, we give up. Tell us already!"

"Since you asked: bridges were covered so horses could cross even if it was icy in the area. The first history lesson is free—the next one will cost you."

The car was parked in the picnic area by the old historic site. Shane, too excited to use the door, stood up, swung his leg over, and jumped out. "Erin, Marty, come here. I'll show you something you've never seen, not even in Big Sky Country."

Shane pointed where the waters met. "This is the

only place in the U.S. where a river flows into a creek. Look—Roaring River, you could jump it, while Crabtree Creek is fourty feet wide. Doesn't make sense, does it?"

Erin asked, "Why call this Roaring River? It's not roaring, nor a river."

"That's the $64,000 question," Shane replied. "Maybe the namer was optimistic. Maybe Roaring River was larger back then. Stick  with me—there's more history and geography to learn."

"Wow, do we have to pay for tour guide lessons? Will there be a test later, maybe a pop quiz?" Marty joked.

"Then, you go first," Shane grinned, winking at Thomas. They tackled Marty. Shane executed a swift single-leg takedown.

Thomas grabbed his arms. "Time for a dunk. We're the dunkers, you're the dunkee."

"Stay in 'till your lips are purple," Kosy added. Marty's hitting the water under the bridge sent rainbow trout scattering with his involuntary splash.

When Marty finally broke the surface to gasp for air, Erin teased, "There's a thin line between smart and smart aleck, Marty. You crossed it."

Shane gripped the rope and swung out over the water, cannonballing Marty for a grand finale. The teens filled the hour with noisy, splashing fun under the covered bridge.

Before another cannonball, Shane called to Erin, "When Kosy and I swim here alone, we feel like we own the place. In Linn County, the clearest streams reveal silver flashes as rainbow trout chase worms on hooks. Fried trout, six to eight inches long, are the best to eat."

That desire to go fishing never left Shane, no matter how far he wandered. The Woods family often caught their limit, storing fish in Wimpy's freezer for winter meals.

Besides the covered bridge, Roaring River Fish Hatchery was the only other tourist attraction in Linn County. The fish hatchery 

has many large concrete tanks that hold thousands of fish, ranging from little fingerlings (minnows) to twenty-six-inchers.

The next stop was this very fish hatchery, as Shane had promised. After they arrived, he began leading the group in his best tour guide voice. Shane pointed to the tank with the medium-sized trout. "There are more than 3,000 fish in this tank. I know, 'cause I counted 'em twice."

"And just how does our tour guide count such a large number of fish?" an inquisitive tourist asked.

"That's easy," the tour guide answered. "Just count their eyes and divide by two!"

"Seriously, Shane," Erin asked, "what do they do with all these fish?"

Shane was standing on the edge of the tank that held the six to eight-inchers. "The ones about this size are put in a truck and dumped in the rivers around here. It is called 'stocking.' Usually they stock the rivers in the spring, giving the fish plenty of time to adapt before the muddy waters of winter ruin their radar.

"Here at the fish hatchery, the water must be cool and constantly running, or these fish will die. These rainbow trout are raised from eggs. The big ones provide the eggs used to hatch the tiny minnows."

Shane then moved to a smaller tank close to the office. "In this tank, you'll find the famous sturgeons. It's from these mighty freshwater monsters that those tasty fish eggs are extracted. Whoever can aford it, enjoys them as caviar."

Erin looked sick. "Yuck! You mean people eat fish eggs? May I never be able to aford it."

"If I don't like your biology lesson, are you going to throw me to them?" Marty asked as he moved away from the edge of the tank.

Kosy tapped Shane on the shoulder. "That guy over there must be partially crippled. Shane, look at the way he is walking into the woods." Kosy noticed no one paid any attention to her.

When one of the workers threw food into the tank that held the medium-sized trout, the water went from a tranquil scene to a frothing, splashing mess. It looked like a TV documentary from the Amazon River in Brazil, with piranhas going berserk.

"May our tour guide please inform us how all this is financed?" Marty asked in his best tourist voice.

The tour guide continued, "Resident fishermen pay five dollars a year for a license, while non-residents pay twenty. That money stocks the rivers with rainbow trout. When the truck comes up Snow Peak Road, we grab our poles and can catch our limit of six in minutes, sometimes without bait. Each fish must be at least six inches, or there's a hefty fine if the game warden catches you."

Erin had one more question. "Do you know anyone who has been caught and fined?"

"Not for undersized fish, but for more than the legal limit, yes," Thomas added. "There are only three game wardens for all of Linn County, which has two thousand three hundred square miles of land. They can hardly cover all the streams and rivers. They're mostly concerned with poaching—hunting or fishing out of season."

Kosy wasn't paying much attention as she had

heard all this before. She was still watching the poor, disabled boy. "Thomas, I don't understand it. Every time that boy goes over to the woods, he walks like a disabled person, but when he comes back, he strolls along quickly, without a limp. Is he disabled or not?"

Now, both Thomas and Shane started paying attention to their sister. Shane began to watch the boy closely, using his peripheral vision so as not to be obvious. "Don't look directly at him, or he'll quickly become suspicious. Let's observe him for a while. Maybe we can catch a poacher." They all made sure to keep a discreet eye on the suspect.

The boy walked to the side of the tank holding the twelve-inch fish. After waiting a few minutes, he walked awkwardly into the woods, disappearing for a time. Then, he reappeared walking normally. Thomas was already onto the kid's trick. "Kosy, go get Mr. Burggraff, the attendant. We'll keep our eyes on this guy. Something stinks around here, and it isn't the fish this time."

Kosy returned with Mr. Burggraff. His forehead ran from above his eyebrows to the middle of his head. His glasses, which must have been made from the bottoms of two Coke bottles, kept slipping down his nose. "What's going on, Thomas? By the way, good to see you kids again. I hope you're here to stay this time."

"Don't look directly at him," Thomas suggested. "But, do you see that kid in the baggy pants and red t-shirt? I think he's hooking fish and dropping them in the woods. Let's let him put one more up his pant leg, and then we'll follow him to the trees."

Kosy and Erin had a hard time restraining their laughter as they caught glances of the kid pulling a large trout up his pant leg. They could hardly believe someone would be that nervy and crude.

"Apparently, he has a line that runs down those loose pants," Marty surmised. "He probably doesn't even need bait. These fish would strike at anything small in the water."

"Oh, yuck," Kosy said, "Can you imagine pulling a slimy, wiggling, cold fish up your pant leg?" She shook her head violently and shuddered.

When the kid began his duck walk back to the trees, Mr. Burggraff and the others advanced towards him. Noticing he was drawing a crowd, the poacher dropped the line and struck out for the deep woods.

They were unable to catch him, but they recovered the fish. Mr. Burggraff was obviously upset. "Grab the ones still wiggling and throw them into the tank. The dead ones, you kids can take home for supper. Can you imagine that? I've worked here for ten years and never seen such a thing."

"Do you know who he is, Mr. Burggraff?" Shane asked as he picked up a flopping trout and headed straight for the big tank.

"No, but if I ever see him again, I'll recognize him and he'll be taken to the police station in Lebanon."

An hour later, on the way back to the Rocking L Ranch, Kosy made a suggestion. "Why don't we go to town? I want one of those blackberry milkshakes at Dairy Queen. They're so thick you can turn them upside down and not a drop will come out." Her suggestion mustered a majority vote, so the '51 Chevy made the trip into Lebanon.

Pulling into the Dairy Queen across from the junior high, they noticed several empty spots. Shane pulled the rustic-looking, shaved-top Chevy alongside a well-kept '56 Ford Fairlane. He grabbed the mike, ordering five extra-thick, wild mountain blackberry milkshakes.

Erin snickered as she whispered to Shane, "Do you suppose that's really that kid's name printed on the driver's door? He's got to be kidding—Engelbert Farnsworth the THIRD."

"It wouldn't surprise me, Erin," Shane replied. "I know that Mr. Farnsworth, who must be the SECOND, is the owner of Cent-Wise Drug store on Main Street, and president of First National Bank."

The five rowdy teens in the Ford were looking for trouble. They noticed the California plates, which Shane hadn't changed yet, and of course, the missing roof. The driver yelled over to Erin, who was staring at them. "Looks like your California special was made into a convertible by a low-hanging overpass."

Erin didn't like these boys from the start. "By the way,

it was a custom job, done by a log truck driver. Do you think he's good enough to open up his own convertible top business?"

"Watch it, Erin. Those guys are bigger than we are. They also outnumber us," Shane warned her.

"So, some real California beach bums, huh?" came the remark from the back seat of the Ford. "Yah, your mudder wears combat boots."

Now it was Thomas's turn. "Not since she was honorably discharged from the Green Berets, she doesn't."

It was Thomas's answer that emptied the Ford. Soon, the 'Bluebird' was surrounded by five angry customers with no good intentions. The tallest one was the driver. He stepped up to Shane's door and looked threatening.

Shane swallowed hard as he prayed silently. The rough bunch grabbed for the doorknob, just as the waitress rolled out on her skates, balancing the order on a large tray. She was definitely inclined to prevent a scrimmage that the owners wouldn't want at the drive-in. "Why don't you five thugs get back in your car and leave these nice kids alone. They look like they just survived an accident?"

With that suggestion, five dissatisfied customers retreated to the Ford. "We'll get you guys later. This is a car no one could miss," the driver responded.

Kosy leaned forward and tapped Shane on the shoulder, "Hey, Brother, that kid driving the car is the same one who was pulling the large trout up his jeans at the fish hatchery."

Shane looked intently at the driver. "I believe you're right, Little Sister. How about you guys, what do you think?" They all agreed he was the same kid.

The girl hooked the tray on the window. "I'm Linda McCarn. What's your name, you handsome guy?"

"I'm … ah … my name is … ah … Shane Woods. Nice to meet you, Linda. Thanks for running off those thugs. They certainly were rude. I'm not looking forward to going to high school with them. Do you know them? Maybe I'll be lucky—tell me they go to Albany High!"

Linda began handing the milkshakes to the three in the back seat. "No such luck, Shane. I know every one of them by name. Every high school has its bullies. I don't let them push me around. Most of the time, they're not so brave when they're alone. That was Engelbert Farnsworth the THIRD. He's a regular pain around here."

Thomas gave Linda a good once-over. "You wouldn't per-chance be the Linda McCarn who went to the Queen Anne Elementary School, would you?"

"Yes, by the way, I'm that Linda. Do I know you kids?"

"Shane, this is the Linda who lived next to us on Grove Street when we went to Queen Anne School," Thomas declared enthusiastically. "Look how grown up she is now. Isn't she cute?"

"And is this your girlfriend sitting next to you, Shane?" Linda asked, raising her eyebrows. It was obvious she hoped Erin was NOT Shane's girlfriend.

"Well, Erin is a girl and a friend," Shane replied awkwardly.

As Shane and Linda reminisced. Erin felt her blood begin to warm. She gritted her teeth at the thoughts that were running through her mind. Finally, she gave in to her feelings. She tipped Shane's milkshake upside down over his lap. "Kosy said you could turn these over and not a drop would come out." She gave the cup a little squeeze. "Oops! Kosy, you were wrong."

There he sat, in all his glory. Erin had filled Shane's lap with his own milkshake. Shane's lower jaw dropped to his chest. He could hardly believe this, usually calm, Montana cowgirl could do such a thing. When he finally came to his senses, he grabbed the melting hunk of ice cream and deposited it between Erin's beautiful, fiery pigtails.

That set everyone in the car to laughing, and soon there was a milkshake fight between all five of them. They were the losers. The Dairy Queen was the winner, as the Lacomb kids had to order a few more shakes. They laughed all the way home.

This incident seemed to be a new revelation for Shane. He began to see Erin had another side. He started to express his feelings after he dropped the Lynches off at the Rocking L Ranch. "Thomas, can you imagine what got into Erin?"

Thomas could hardly believe Shane couldn't interpret Erin's actions. "Come on, Shane. You mean to tell me you really don't know why Erin dumped your milkshake in your lap?"

Shane started scratching his head. "Could it be possible Erin was actually jealous of Linda?" He had no experience with girls. He moved around so much he never developed a close friendship with either boys or girls. He hoped with all his heart those transient days were all behind him, history for sure.

Thomas was shaking his head at his naive younger brother. "Only a dunderhead could miss that conclusion, Shane!"

The kid with the ice cream stain in his lap was still a little bit in the dark. "I'm not sure if what she did is good news or bad news. But, I'm positive I'll find out soon enough."

7 - A Rundown

The strawberry season was almost over. In a few weeks, only the small, partially green ones would be available to buy. It was now or never to make jam or jelly, freeze them, or can them. The work would not stop in the Linn County harvest fields. Teens who wanted to could earn over $500 during the summer just by working in the berry and bean harvests.

Cherry and pear picking was more hazardous, since pickers had to work with only one hand while hanging onto a branch or ladder

Raspberries, blackcaps, and boysenberries were everywhere in Linn County. Wild blackberries were in ditches, meridians and open fields.

To pick wild blackberries, Shane laid boards into the patch, moving them ahead as he ventured deeper into yellowjacket-spider territory.

Picking blackberries was not a job for timid souls. The yellowjacket spiders fiercely guarded their webs.

Grandma even claimed they jumped at humans, something Kosy believed.

If someone was not up to facing the notorious spiders, they could always grab a few gallon jugs and float down the canal in Lebanon, picking wild blackberries as they enjoyed a summer swim. The only problem with floating the canal was the long walk back upstream.

Shane had experienced it all. He even picked prunes—properly called plums until dried. A prune is just a dried plum. And, in the same way, a raisin is simply a dried grape.

Usually, the pickers could partake of the fruit they were picking, unless it was boysenberries. These rare berries were so big and tart no one could eat many. The owners didn't like the pickers eating the berries because their scarcity made them very valuable—expensive, to boot!

For most fruit, eating while picking was a right. Not so with rare boysenberries or too many plums. And no one ate what the owners always kept: garlic.

Shane had picked blackcaps until his hands were stained for weeks. He had even hoed the mint fields for a dollar an hour. Carrying two five-gallon cans of water, he had provided irrigation for young, tender tomato plants. That was when he was only eleven years old.

These experiences were routine for anyone in Linn County, as normal as fishing in Crabtree Creek or swinging under covered bridges. Oregonians took them for granted and loved their way of life.

Who would trade the crystal clear water of Crabtree Creek or the smoke-free air of Linn County for the pollution of an enormous city, where you didn't feel safe even with the doors locked and barred? This was living at its best. It was a great place to raise a family.

After reflecting on all these memories, Shane stopped at the Rocking L Ranch on his way into town. The shift from his thoughts to his actions was sudden, but familiar. He jumped over the car door rather than opening it. That had been his new custom since the logging truck had turned 'Bluebird' into a permanent convertible.

Erin was peeking through her bedroom window and enjoying the scene. Shane had no sooner entered the front room before the Montana cowgirl grabbed his hand and whisked him out the back door. She motioned for him to sit on the picnic bench.

"I have something on my mind," she started a bit nervously, tugging at her perfectly webbed pigtail. "I'd like to apologize for dumping your milkshake in your lap last night. That was a stupid thing to do, and I don't even want to think about why I did it. Will you forgive me for that?"

Shane was trying to keep cool. That was his usual mode of operation. He was forcing himself to retain a sober face. Inside, he was smiling to beat the band and enjoying every word. He hiked his bottom lip up over his top lip to keep from revealing his genuine emotions.

"I certainly will, my good friend. Needless to say, you caught me quite by surprise. Is that all you want to say to me?" He was hopefully probing for more information about her true feelings towards him. But, alas, they were not forthcoming just yet. Erin answered negatively and excused herself.

After he left Erin's house, Shane had a lot to ponder as he drove into town to visit Bowie. The interaction with Erin still lingered in his mind, but his focus began to shift to his new friend and the questions that came with their budding friendship.

He wanted to learn from Bowie, who was proud of his Nez Perce heritage. Maybe Shane could even discover more about his own roots by learning from his friend.

If he were lucky, Shane hoped he might share his beliefs with Bowie someday. He had learned Spanish from friends in California, but learning Nez Perce wasn't on his mind, yet.

Driving alone down Lacomb Road, Shane descended from the highest point and spotted Brewster's Corner ahead. Though he rarely traveled solo, he enjoyed these moments to reflect on his new Christian life and the decisions before him.

He was still deep in thought, so he didn't notice the white '55 Chevy catching up to him. It passed him like a shot. He just shrugged his shoulders as to who it was. The Chevy, with the bad paint job, slowed down, inviting him to pass. Shane got that nervous, butterflies-in-the-stomach feeling. He passed the car anyway. Uh-oh, trouble!

It was already too late when Shane realized the white Chevy belonged to the Snow Peak robbers. Worse than that, they also recognized him. Shane's smaller engine was not going to be a match for their powerful V-8. But what else could he do except make a run for it?

They quickly closed the gap. Shane saw Horace, the boss, driving. He couldn't believe the robbers were ramming him. "They must want to run me off the road and wreck my car—and who knows what after that?" Worst-case scenarios raced through his mind, a result of his choleric personality, he often told himself.

A Mercury came into view at the next crossing. To avoid trouble, the white '55 Chevy slowed down, playing innocent as both Chevys passed the intersection. The Mercury entered the road and advanced, passing both cars. This was Shane's chance to tailgate, the only means of safety he had. The new car sped up, and Shane stayed right on its tail light.

No one likes tailgaters. Shane tried to get the couple's attention, even motioning for them to stop. The elderly Lacomb couple was 

not inclined to give credence to teens, especially in homemade convertibles. They didn't like his tailing that close, so they sped up and left Shane to the mercy of the white plague behind him.

Panic flared through Shane's mind and muscles. He felt the blood rush from the surface of his skin. "I won't make it to Brewster's Corner before they knock me in the ditch. I can't out-run'm, so I'll have to outsmart'm."

He was still two hundred yards ahead of them. His smaller motor was getting hotter by the minute. He spied a wide gravel driveway on the right—just enough room for a spin around. Still at a reasonable speed, he hit the gravel, jerking his steering wheel tight to the left—a perfect donut. Spinning completely around, he threw gravel all over the road. The dust had not cleared before he hit the pavement again and headed straight for the robbers.

'Bluebird' propelled down the left lane straight for the '55 Chevy. It wasn't a form of 'chicken' because Shane was counting on the notion that these crooks were actually cowards at heart. He wasn't the bravest person in the world himself, but, in these short minutes, he could not see any other alternative.

The white car stood its ground. With only one hundred yards between them now, space was getting to be a premium. The robbers WERE cowards. Horace, the biggest coward, was driving. "Getting even with dat smart-aleck kid isn't worth wrecking our car."

The Woods kid slowed down to about 25 miles per hour, but maintained his position in their lane, heading straight for them, his hands, bloodlessly tight, gripped the steering wheel.

Speed was not necessary. He just wanted to get past them and back to Lacomb. Now Shane could actually see the contortions on their surprised, stupid faces.

They could not believe HE was attacking THEM. "It's now or never," Shane thought. He wasn't going to give in to these crooks. With lots of commotion in the front seat, the robbers finally swerved around Shane, almost shooting into the ditch. As soon as they regained control of the car, they hit the gravel Shane had thrown on the road when he turned around. That slide DID put them in the ditch.

The grappler took advantage of his excellent opportunity to return to Lacomb and safety. The last he saw of the robbers, they were pushing their car out of the ditch, heading into town, obviously looking for more trouble to perpetrate on hapless victims.

This was a good time for a Thanksgiving prayer. "Thank you, Lord, for helping this foolhardy, inexperienced driver." Since he accepted Christ, Shane had discovered prayer was not just a nightly 'Now-I-lay-me-down-to-sleep' ritual. It was a call for assistance or a thankful communication with God, through Christ, at any time he needed to.

Shane had a good story to tell Sergeant Kochian when he talked to the policeman from Erin's house. Although still a bit nervous, Shane managed to carry on a conversation. "It's apparent the robbers are still using the '55 Chevy. Do you think they'll dump it soon, Sergeant?"

"These hoodlums won't leave our county until they've tapped all the resources available. I'll keep my ears open for any reports of stolen cars. I think they'll rid themselves of that car soon. It's been seen too many times. Keep me informed if you see them again."

"I was glad no one was with me. I don't think I would've done what I did if even one other person had been in the car. It's one thing to make such a serious decision for yourself, but quite another to make it for someone else. I'll check in with you later, Sergeant."

Shane finally relaxed, sitting down in the well-worn armchair. "What could happen to me next?" he thought to himself. Adventure was one thing, but coming this close to a head-on collision was not his idea of an adventure that was well planned. Maybe he could get a job as a stunt driver when he got out of high school!

"Lunch will be ready soon," Erin promised. "You and Kosy will certainly stay, won't you?"

"Yeah, we can stay," Shane affirmed, "But why is everyone around here grinning like the cat in 'Alice in Wonderland?' Do you all know something I don't, but should?" He had already discovered it was best to park his life on the side of caution when dealing with Erin and Marty.

Nobody gave him a straight answer. It was eating time again at the Lynch Ranch. Sitting down at their kitchen table was something Shane had happily accustomed himself to enjoy. He had never been disappointed with the food, and didn't expect to be this time either. Things might be a little different at this meal. Mr. and Mrs. Lynch had gone into town, leaving the kitchen to the kids. Erin opened the refrigerator door. "What's this green, hairy stuff growing in here?"

Marty and Erin were making the best of it for Shane's benefit. "It looks like Dad's letting the cheese mold to make Roquefort dressing. Shall we whip up some now and serve it to Shane?"

Shane's fears were well-founded. "Hey, you guys, I'm not eating anything out of the ordinary while Mrs. Lynch is absent from the kitchen. Not that I don't trust you, but I like to play it safe when it comes to something as important as my stomach. I don't want any peaches with worms."

They sat down at the table, and before anyone was asked to say the blessing, Erin brought in a covered plate. "Hey, what's this?" Shane burst out as he scratched his head. "It looks like your mother's fanciest silver plate and cover. We must be going to have pheasant under glass or some other, exotic foreign dish."

"We'll give you the pleasure, Shane," Marty

invited him to take the lid off the plate. "The honor is yours."

Shane always enjoyed being honored, especially by such a good group of close friends. He raised the lid, and before he could even get a good look at what it was, IT leaped up and landed on his chest. Bounding away again, it cleared the entire living room and stopped, squatting on the couch. Erin, true to her form, jumped up on the kitchen table.

Shane was so startled he dropped the lid. "What ... what in the world are you guys laughing at? That CRITTER almost scared me to death."

"It's not a CRITTER, Shane," Kosy explained. "It's just a harmless bullfrog. We were out by the barn and kept hearing this loud sound like 'jug-o-rum, jug-o-rum,' so Marty started lifting planks until he found our smooth-skinned, yellow-and-black-striped friend. What do you think of him? We were really impressed with how far he could jump."

"Marty thinks he has possibilities at the frog jumping contest in Corvallis," Erin added, from her perch on the table.

"I'm surprised a girl who won't have anything to do with a slimy worm would play around with a leaping, slimy frog," Shane complained to the girl crouched on the table.

"Who said I even touched him?" Erin replied, defending her femininity. "Marty and Kosy did all the dirty work; I just continued to cheer them on."

"If you think for one minute I'm going to forget this practical joke, you're all very wrong. I'll find a way to personally get even with each one of you, including the frog," Shane promised with an evil grin on his usually innocent face. "In fact, if we keep that frog long enough, he might have possibilities of filling a frying pan with those big, powerful legs of his."

Marty was horrified. "You're not going to eat Leaping Larry, are you? He has a lot of blue ribbons in those ham hocks."

"Yeah, and the final ribbon will be won at the Linn County Hot Dish Contest," Shane added as he hurried to retrieve the slippery, elusive, slimy Leaping Larry.

*The famous, elusive, slimy "Leaping Larry"
is sitting on a silver platter.*

8 - Nez Perce History

"The single-leg takedown is the most popular, but you must also learn the duck under, the fireman's carry, and the double-leg takedown. The ankle grab is good, too, but it's just a lower form of the single-leg takedown." Marty was giving Shane his second wrestling lesson.

Double Leg Takedown

"For every move there's a countermove. You also need to learn the counter moves. Let's work on the single-leg takedown for thirty minutes. That'll probably be your bread and butter. What weight do you suppose you'll wrestle?"

"What do you think?" Shane was trying to pinch an inch on his hips.

Marty assessed Shane. "With your frame, wrestle at 141 or 136 pounds. Build muscle, lose some fat, then pick a weight class. Watch your food—cut out ice cream and pie."

"Well, if I keep getting my milkshakes served in my lap, I won't have to worry about those calories," Shane joked. While Marty became distracted by the humor, Shane seized the chance: he reached down, grabbed Marty's right knee with one hand, and used his leg to kick Marty's left ankle out from under him. Marty lost his balance and landed on his back. Shane grinned and asked, "Were you on your back long enough to count all the ceiling tiles, my dear instructor?"

Marty was impressed. "Shane, if you work hard in an hour's practice, you can easily lose five to six pounds, IF the humidity and temperature are kept high." Marty adjusted his headgear.

"You should wear headgear all the time, even in practice, unless you want cauliflower ears. Girls don't like cauliflower ears."

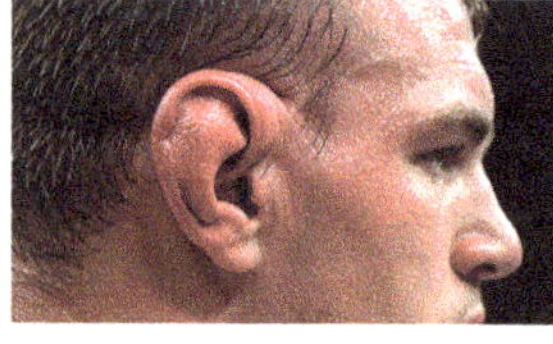

"Then give me a headgear, please," Shane insisted.

"I have some bad news for you, Shane," Marty frowned. "I was asking around. I even phoned Coach Hazewinkle, and my fears were confirmed. Can you imagine who wrestles at 141 pounds for the Warriors?"

"Well, considering who I know in town, it must be Engelbert Farnsworth the THIRD, or it wouldn't be significant news. But, how could that be? He's at least six feet tall. He looked like he weighed at least 170 pounds."

Marty opened the weight room door. "You're right! But he's so 'gung ho' he sacrifices to reach 141 pounds. He even uses a sauna at home." Hearing this, Shane grew nervous. To distract himself, he began lifting weights, pushing until he tired.

"Easy, Shane," Marty warned. "Use lighter weights and more reps for cable strength, not bulk."

Shane set down the dumbbell. "Want to go to town and see Bowie? Maybe grab a Basket Special at Richie's—burger, fries, Coke for fifty cents. Maybe a milkshake before I join Eaters Anonymous."

Erin considered whether it was wise to take Shane's car, knowing the trouble it had already attracted from the Snow Peak robbers and Engelbert Farnsworth III. Eventually, she conceded her point. "It's either Shane's car or we stay home. Riding the horses would take too long, so let's get going."

Summer nights in Linn County could be very hot and humid. Some kids can't stand to sleep in a hot house, so they throw a sleeping bag on the lawn and tell jokes until the mosquitoes drive them into their sacks. On a night like this, the '51 Chevy trooped into Lebanon, top down (their only choice), and the friends began their adventure together.

Arriving in Lebanon, they pulled into the T.P. Oil Company gas station. Shane parked the car behind the office to keep it out of sight. Inside, Bowie was at the desk. As they entered, Kosy paused, drawn to a large picture on the wall. "Who's that, Bowie?"

"I was hoping you would ask," Bowie answered proudly. "That's Chief Joseph of the Nez Perce Tribe.

He was considered the greatest military strategist of all the Native American chiefs."

This was the information Shane was looking for, and he thought Bowie was just the right person to fill them in on the Nez Perce. "Tell us about your people, Bowie."

"Well, first let me tell you about my family. I have twin sisters in the eighth grade at the junior high. One is White Dove Pinetree, and the other is Running Fawn Pinetree. I'll introduce them to you later. I also have an older brother, Bear Claw Pinetree, who's currently studying at Oregon State University.

"We got our name from the French. It means 'pierced nose,' for which I have yet to find out the reason. I have an idea it really means 'flat nose,' like the one I have." With that, he put his index finger on his nose and laid it flat against his cheekbone.

"My grandfather was a full-blooded Cherokee," Shane added. "Since I never met him, I know little about his life. What's your connection with Chief Joseph?"

"Chief Joseph was my great-grandfather," Bowie began explaining. "We used to live on the Nez Perce reservation in Northern Idaho. But there were too many descendants of Chief Joseph. It was becoming a situation of too many chiefs and not enough Indians.

"Reservation life leaves a lot to be desired. My dad figured that boat wouldn't float. So, he decided to come here, where we could have a normal life without depending on a monthly government handout."

"So that makes Chief Joseph your dad's grandfather," Erin stated with admiration. "Wow, that's really something! We've heard a lot about Chief Joseph. There were many Nez Perce in our area of Montana."

Bowie finally had someone to share with. "Chief Joseph tried to live peacefully with settlers. He attended a mission school and learned tactics by observing soldiers. When conflict arose, he ordered a retreat, knowing the Army outmatched them."

The Nez Perce teenager walked over to the picture, ready to add detail. "Chief Joseph of the Nez Perce in Oregon believed in forbearance. He said. 'Better to live in peace than to begin a war and lie dead.' Despite his peaceful nature, he was forced off his land.

"His retreat toward Canada is often called one of history's most brilliant military maneuvers, but he was captured forty miles short of the border and spent the rest of his life on a reservation in Colville, Washington, where he died in 1904."

"How is it that you know so much about Nez Perce history?" Kosy asked.

"Well, my Little White Princess," Bowie said as he stood up and towered over Kosy, "I've made it my hobby, Native American history, and not just MY tribe. I also know something about the great Cherokee Nation. But, right now, I have to be excused to attend to a very impatient customer."

Bowie serviced the car and returned, scowling. When he rounded his desk, he slammed his fist down so hard the whole office vibrated. "That was old knucklehead again. He knows I'm a Native American, and always makes wisecracks. I think his dad owns a store here in town."

"That wouldn't be old Engelbert Farnsworth the THIRD, would it?" Thomas asked. "I think I recognize the car and your very colorful description of him."

"Yeah, that's him. Do you know him personally? Is he a friend of yours?" Bowie hoped both answers would be negative.

Hearing Bowie's question, everyone in the room laughed together, their amusement easing the mood.

"Not exactly," Shane answered, "but we do know him. Actually, I don't think Bert could have any real friends."

Amid the lull in the conversation, a deep growl suddenly rang out in the room. Kosy was the first to react, wrinkling her forehead in confusion. She turned to the others and asked, "Was that a bear or a German Shepherd I just heard growling?"

Marty had not been fooled by the sound. Recognizing it, he said with a grin, "That was one big guy's empty stomach, right, Bowie?" This reminded Marty of their real reason for stopping at the T. P. station.

"Say, Bowie, can you go to Richie's Drive-in with us to get a hamburger?" Marty asked, hoping for a positive answer.

"Sure, I'd love to. Wait just five minutes more, and my dad will be here to replace me. I'm sure he'll let me go. There's only one thing I like better than hamburgers—that's PIZZA!"

Marty never missed a chance to practice his investigative skills. "Just by chance, would you happen to be a wrestler, Bowie?"

"What makes you ask that?"

"It's the size of your neck," Marty revealed his hint. "Most wrestlers have thick necks from neck bridging. It also means when they buy a shirt that fits them well on the neck, the sleeves usually drag on the ground."

Bowie continued, "I've had two years of wrestling experience in junior high. I like the rodeo, too. I guess a love of horses is in my blood. The Nez Perce were excellent horsemen. They developed the Appaloosa, selling many to the U.S. Cavalry.

"There's a rodeo in John Day and several roundups before school starts. The big one is the second week of September. It's called the Pendleton Roundup. I go every year. Maybe you guys could go with me sometime, to be my cheering section."

Shane was sure they could. "What do you know about my tribe, the Cherokee Nation?"

"Well, the Cherokee Nation started on the East Coast, in the Carolinas. They were the first literate tribe. The humorist, Will Rogers, was part Cherokee," Bowie explained.

"They lived as farmers in the Southern Appalachian Mountains, and sided with the British during America's War for Independence. Both of our tribes suffered the same fate. When gold was discovered on the land the U.S. Government gave them, they were run off and relocated elsewhere. The unfortunate Cherokees were marched on foot to Indian Territory, which is now Oklahoma. The Nez Perce tribe was herded into Northern Idaho.

"The greatest athlete of all time was Cherokee. Jim Thorpe won the decathlon and pentathlon in the 1912 Olympics, played professional baseball, and professional football. No other American has done that. He was also one of the founders of the National Football League. Well, here's my dad. I guess we can go now."

After lengthy introductions and a few friendly pats on the back, the '51 Chevy pulled out, heading up Park Street. Shane wanted to drag the Main before ending up at Richie's Drive-in. Shane stopped at the red light on Grant Street. A 1961 Corvette convertible pulled up next to him, revving the powerful engine to a competition level.

Shane leaned out the window. "You've got to be kidding, you want to drag down Main Street?"

The driver shouted over the roar of his motor. "These are both Chevrolets, made by the same company, right?"

"Sure," Erin yelled back. "But your rubber band is wound much tighter than ours."

"Yeah, forget it," Shane echoed. "We don't drag, ever. That would be reckless and irresponsible."

The irate driver angled his head out the window and yelled, "Who are you anyway, Goody two-shoes? Come on! Let's have some fun." In his unsaved state, Shane would have been perturbed enough to take the challenge. But it still would not have made any difference. His car against a Corvette, are you kidding? It would be like the turtle and the hare, but in this case, the turtle would not win.

He was different now. It wouldn't be a good testimony for a Christian to be dragging down Main Street, or anywhere else. Christ certainly had made a difference in Shane's life. The wildness was gone. A sense of gratitude to his Savior had replaced it. Shane still felt neutral about his mom, but he was a new Christian yet. Things like that would change eventually as well.

Shane just wrinkled up his nose and waved goodbye to the dragster. "No way, Jose, endangering my car and my passengers is not my idea of fun."

Just then, the light turned green, and the Corvette peeled out, fishtailing for about ten yards. Marty couldn't help himself. "The tire companies' best friend. He probably gets five per gallon, if he's lucky."

"Well, five miles per gallon isn't bad for a Corvette," Thomas wanted to show his intelligence.

"Miles! I'm talking about five blocks per gallon," Marty snickered. Shane did not repent for holding back. Besides the fact that he would have looked ridiculous, there were always police cars just waiting for teens to 'drag' the Main. Shane felt he could drag the Main without 'dragging' the Main.

The Woods kid was not a prophet nor the son of a prophet. But just as the Corvette passed Maple Street, a squad car pulled out behind it and turned on a flashing red light.

As the '51 Chevy snuck by the Corvette, Erin could not help herself. She stuck her head out of what should have been a convertible roof and yelled, "We'll beat you after all. Oh, good evening, Sergeant Kochian. I hope Lois is well!"

9 - A Setup

Richie's Drive-in is a favorite hangout for Lebanon teens, especially during lunch hour on school days. Shane had heard all about rush-hour traffic. He already had his strategy worked out.

At the end of his fourth hour class, IF he was sitting close to the door and could leave his books with a friend, so he wouldn't have to return to his locker and fight with a stubborn combination, he could be among the first ones out of the building.

IF he didn't let anyone pass him and hightailed it a little, he could make it to Richie's to enjoy a Basket Special for lunch. Even after taking a few spins on the chair, he would still have time to walk back to school to catch fifth hour. But all that would be unnecessary. Shane was lucky enough to have a '51 Chevy convertible. He could go in style without getting all sweaty.

All these thoughts filled his mind as he opened the door to Richie's and smelled the hamburgers frying. Finding six empty stools in a row at Richie's was next to impossible, so the Woods, Lynch, and Pinetree gang sat in a booth. Unfortunately, they were not concerned about the car. They didn't see the '56 Ford pull up beside it.

The Lacomb gang didn't take notice of Bert until he and his buddies had already pulled out onto the highway. They were not so coy as to have escaped entirely unnoticed. Shane was the first to rise and head for the door. "Those guys just came out of the parking lot. I don't trust them. I'll be right back. I'm going to check the car. Watch my hamburger."

When he returned, all of the clowns at the booth were leaning over, staring at Shane's sandwich. "Okay, I get the point. You can stop gawking at my supper."

"Well, Shane," Kosy smiled, "you did ask us to watch it, right?"

"Yeah, I did, but next time you don't have to take me quite so literally. I didn't see anything wrong with the car. They certainly couldn't take a knife to the top."

Fifty cents wasn't bad for a supper. When a teen only made a dollar an hour, they had to work for 30 minutes to pay for a Basket Special. Therefore, it was still a Dutch treat most of the time. No one could afford to be overly generous.

When they pulled out of Richie's, Shane headed for the station to drop Bowie off at work. First, they decided to drag the Main one more time. Gas was only twelve cents a gallon; they could afford a little frivolity if everyone pitched in a nickel!

Stopping at the light on Grant Street, Shane put the car in neutral, a bad habit he was about to break. The '56 Ford pulled up behind him, bumping his car. Engelbert Farnsworth III did not stop there. He pushed Shane right into the intersection.

The car turning left onto Main Street had to come to a sudden, screeching stop. The innocent teens in the blue Chevy were severely reprimanded by a couple of senior citizens who were ignorant of the real culprits. Shane gave them a sheepish grin and quickly passed through the intersection to clear the traffic.

The bad news was not over. A policeman had witnessed only the near accident; he had not seen what Bert did. He pulled Shane over to the side as Engelbert Farnsworth III and his rowdies passed, thumbing their noses at the unlucky bunch.

"Let's have all of you kids out of the car and up against the building," the officer ordered. "We received an anonymous call informing us of a blue '51 Chevy convertible full of teens who were drinking."

Thomas was indignant. "Well, that's not us. No one in this car drinks, ever. We all hate liquor with a passion." This was not a joke; no Woods kid ever spoke well of any form of liquor. They had seen their mother use all types of it, and every drop of it had ruined their lives and driven their mother into hiding.

"We'll see," the officer promised. "Just take it easy while I search this car."

Erin was a bit put out and nervously twirled her pigtail. "He won't find anything. How could he find any alcohol?" Kosy was munching on her fingernails. Shane was stroking his chin, and Marty's knee was starting its nervous twitch.

The officer didn't take much time to search the car. He seemed to know right where it was. He looked in the faces of six petrified teens when he held up a half-empty bottle of whiskey. "You kids will have to come with me to the station. I'm new here, so I'll trust you to follow me."

Thomas got behind the wheel and tried to calm the troops. Everyone was casting puzzled glances at each other. The what-do-we-do-now look permeated the place.

Bowie was the first to speak. "I know it was that bunch in the '56 Ford. It had to be old Engelbert Farnsworth the THIRD, and his buddies—the group with room temperature IQ's. I can't wait until I get my hands on them. They'll be lucky if I don't put sugar in their gas tank." With that, he vented his frustrations by slamming his fist into his open palm. This was no teen to trifle with; he was angry and had the muscle and weight to back up his threat.

At the station, the atmosphere changed in favor of the '51 Chevy group. The other officers, having followed Shane's actions since he relocated to Lacomb, were not in the least inclined to believe the setup.

Johnathan Hitz, the officer working the graveyard shift, quickly vouched for them, as well as Sergeant

Kochian. "Just smell their breath and let them go," the secretary suggested. "These kids are as innocent as morning glories."

"I hope none of this will get in the paper," Erin requested politely. "We don't need that kind of publicity." Erin was always deeply concerned about her Christian testimony. She wanted to shine for Christ even as a teenager.

It wasn't a story they wanted circulated; therefore, at church on Sunday, no one even mentioned it. Pastor John Ballentine stopped Shane in the foyer. "Have you been reading the Gospel of John like I suggested? You know you have to study the Bible, not just tuck it under your pillow at nighttime, hoping to learn something by osmosis!"

Shane liked this elderly pastor. "Yes, I've been studying the Book, and I find it very interesting. You know, the first time I ever read the Bible, I started in Matthew and got bogged down in the 'begats.' I wasn't impressed. I quit before I finished the first chapter. But now I really understand more about Christ and what He expects of me."

The pastor was very pleased with Shane's progress. "Keep your eyes and ears open, Shane. You'll find that God will speak a great deal to you through His Word. There's no limit to what He can do through a surrendered vessel."

The new convert was encouraged by Pastor Ballentine's interest in his spiritual growth. Shane lowered his voice. "Please keep praying for Thomas and Kosy. I really want them to get saved, too. I don't know how to answer Kosy's questions about Mom. Maybe you can come up with an answer she can accept; something that will help."

Pastor Ballentine gave Shane a winning smile and a warm pat on the back. "I'll work on that problem and put it at the top of my prayer list. I know how you kids have suffered, and I believe I can help Kosy." With that, the kind pastor turned to Thomas. "What are your plans for this lovely summer afternoon?"

Thomas answered the pastor and caught the Lynches' attention simultaneously. "We're going to the covered bridge to swim. Would you two Lynches like to come along? Maybe we could even scare a few crayfish."

Marty talked to his parents. Mrs. Lynch had a better idea. "Why don't you three come to our house for lunch, and then go swimming from there? We have lots of food just waiting to be devoured. And you guys look like the crew that could do the job."

Thomas conferred with Grandpa and Grandma, giving Mrs. Lynch the affirmative sign (fist closed with the thumb up). 

The Lynch kitchen was designed practically. It was circular, with cupboards lining the entire circumference. The wooden circular counter top, six feet in diameter, decorated the center of the room. Mrs. Lynch was cutting strawberries and mixing them with raspberries for shortcake. She looked up when Thomas walked through the door.

"You'll be returning to San Diego soon, right, Thomas? I bet you'll miss your family a lot. Shane and Kosy have become regular attractions around here. They sure have given Marty and Erin good friends to pal around with."

"That's right, Mrs. Lynch," Thomas answered. "I only have four days left. Then the real tough training begins. Did you know that only three in a hundred of the trainees make it through the Navy UDT boot camp?"

Mrs. Lynch looked surprised. "You'll really have to apply yourself, Thomas. I guess you might finally discover what you're made of—MAN OF STEEL! We'll be praying for you and your safety. By the way, right after lunch, I have something to show you kids."

Mr. Lynch said the blessing, and then it was time to attack the table. A bucket of fried chicken, a mountain of mashed potatoes, and tiers of corn on the cob, accompanied by cold lemonade to wash it all down. And to top it all off, a veritable June delight—strawberry/raspberry shortcake.

Mr. Lynch was just diving through the whipped cream when he spoke to Shane. "After the Strawberry Fair is over, are you and Kosy going to continue to work in the harvest fields?"

Shane looked at Kosy first. "We will some, to spend our time wisely. No one will hire a fifteen-year-old. We'll work on the raspberry harvest and then the pole beans. But by next summer, I expect to have a regular job.”

“Come with me, kids,” Mrs. Lynch motioned to the Woods family. “Let the Lynches clear off the table. Behind the barn, we have a chicken mesh pen with some very fine homing pigeons I'd like to show you.

“It is a hobby of mine, but the whole family enjoys it. Every time we go on a long trip, we let one loose to see how long it takes the bird to get home. Sometimes we even send messages tied to their legs. This brown one here is named 'Speedy.' He's my favorite.”

Kosy was careful where she stepped. “What's the longest distance you've tried?”

Mrs. Lynch really appreciated Kosy's question. “That's the most common question asked. Pigeons have been known to fly more than a thousand miles in two days.”

Thomas was amazed. “Wow, that wouldn't leave much time for eating, sleeping, or dating.”

Mrs. Lynch continued, “We've been turning Speedy loose further from home each time. That's the way we train them. The furthest he has flown is from the Idaho border. Each time he beats us home. Enough pigeon lore for today. You had better hurry to the covered bridge since the clouds are getting gray and darker.”

The water was cool, but clear. Marty could see the

crayfish scurrying across the bottom. Under the covered bridge was an area wide enough to push off the rope swing, to do a cannonball, or a feet-first plunge. Headfirst diving would not be smart.

Erin noticed it first. "There's a putrid smell around here."

"I smelled it, too," Thomas agreed, pinching his nose between his fingers. "I think it must be coming from behind those trees over there."

Marty and Shane investigated. Shane held up his hand, motioning for the girls to stay where they were. "It's a doe. Someone has killed and skinned it, taking only the meat. This is the work of poachers. There's probably a young fawn around here wondering what to do now."

Kosy looked concerned. She always had a tender heart for the unfortunate and mistreated because she knew how it felt. "A fawn without its mother, how horrible. If we find the fawn, can we take it to the fish hatchery? Will they be able to save it?"

"Catching a fawn would be like trying to catch the wind," Marty responded. He noticed Kosy's tender heart and wished she would get saved soon.

Trying to Catch the Wind

Thomas wanted to dig a hole to bury the remains. "I hate poaching. Poachers destroy God's handiwork with no regard for the severe consequences. If it can avoid the cougars, bears, and mountain lions around here, the fawn has a chance to survive."

"There are predators around here, for sure," Marty concurred. "Remember the big mountain lion that chased the robber into the river?"

Thomas went to the car and retrieved a shovel. The three boys took turns digging a hole to bury the remains. This would make for a better atmosphere for their swimming adventure. After the dirty work, it was back to fun time. The only thing closer to a Lacomb teenager's heart than swimming in Crabtree Creek was fishing in it.

Most bridges around the area had rope swings if the water was deep enough for plunging. The rock base of this bridge provided a perfect ledge to push off from. It was twelve feet wide and had a seven-foot drop straight to the water.

The rope swing had a loop on the bottom. Kosy grabbed the rope and pushed off with her foot in the loop. Thomas didn't think it was a good idea. "Kosy, take your foot out of the loop. It's ..."

Before he could finish the sentence, Kosy's grip slipped from the rope, and her foot was caught in the loop. Erin screamed as Kosy swung back towards the rock headfirst.

The covered bridge was a delightful place to swim and use the rope to swing off the slab of rock. You can see the rock under the left side.

10 - A Near Drowning

Before she hit the ledge, Kosy was able to cushion herself with her extended arms. She still slammed her head on the rock with a sickening thud, knocking herself unconscious. Her foot slipped out of the loop, and she dropped under the water.

In the fractional moment before horror paralyzed her, Erin managed to squeak out another terrifying scream. Shane was by the car when he witnessed the horrible scene. A violent, instantaneous explosion of absolute terror roared through him. He just stood there with his mouth open.

Thomas yelled at Shane, bringing him back to his senses. "Warm up the car and point it towards Lebanon." All of his Naval training was coming to mind again. He was glad he had paid close attention in all his first-aid classes.

Marty was the first to get close to Kosy. He dove quickly, lifting her from the water. Thomas hit the water running and began mouth-to-mouth resuscitation before Marty could get Kosy to the shore.

Erin was crying and screaming at the same time. Marty

crawled into the back seat, and Thomas followed, still trying to revive his sister. As Shane fishtailed out of the gravel parking lot, Marty was emphatic, "Pedal to the metal, Shane, don't spare the rubber."

Shane was throwing rocks all over the place before he hit the bridge, smoking the back tires on the wooden planks, and praying, "God, please don't let my little sister die. I love her, and she doesn't know Christ as her Savior. Please God, give my sister another chance to be saved, and help us get to the hospital safely."

Thomas was still trying to get Kosy to breathe. "Shane, when you hit Snow Peak Road, turn right. Don't stop at the crossings; use your horn. When we get to Western Plywood, turn left. Don't spare the car."

Shane felt the necessity for hurrying, but the safety of all concerned was also on his mind. "I'll do the best I can, Thomas. I can't go very fast until we get off this gravel. There'd be no sense in wrecking the car and injuring all of us."

Erin was still crying and praying as the Chevy turned onto Snow Peak Road. As Thomas was administering first aid, he could think of a few times he had mistreated his Kosy. Even though he wasn't a Christian, he prayed, "God, please save my sister."

Every moment was crucial. If Kosy didn't start breathing before they reached the plywood mill, she would die. "Hold her head back farther, Marty," Thomas yelled. Kosy began coughing up water, and Thomas sighed with relief as his sister started gasping roughly. "She's going to make it. Man, am I ever glad I didn't sleep through that first aid class! Kosy is still not out of danger, Shane, so keep up the speed, but don't be reckless! How do you feel, Kosy?"

Her pulse pounded fiercely in her temples from the wound on her head, and her chest ached so severely she could hardly breathe. "I ... I feel terrible. My chest feels like ... an elephant is sitting on it."

Murphy's Law was still in effect in Linn County. When Shane passed Brewster's Corner, a red dome began flashing behind him. He was relieved and disappointed at the same time. "These local policemen seem to like my car."

Shane motioned for the squad car to pull alongside. The officer followed his request. "What's the hurry, kid? Where's the fire?"

Motioning to the back seat, Shane shouted at the officer. "We have a medical emergency. My sister is badly hurt. Can you help us? We're going to the hospital emergency room."

"Sure can, kids, follow me," the officer motioned as he pulled out in front, turned on his siren, and left his light flashing. The rest of the trip was easier. Pedestrians and drivers gave them weird looks.

Pulling into the emergency entrance at Lebanon Community Hospital, Thomas released Kosy to the doctors but stayed by her side. He looked at Shane,

"Phone Grandma and Grandpa and tell them where we are."

After Kosy's head injury was treated, she was put in room 106 in the new west wing. Dr. Ferguson put his hand on Thomas' shoulder. "If you hadn't administered first aid procedures, your sister wouldn't have made it. That compress rag on the head also helped. Where did you learn all that medical information? If you want to visit her now, you can."

The happy foursome entered Kosy's room. Shane grabbed her hand. There were tears of joy in his young eyes. "God answered my prayer, Kosy."

"I ... I thought I was going to die, Thomas. I was so scared. Thank you for saving my life. Will Grandpa and Grandma be here soon?"

Kosy stayed overnight in the hospital for observation, but the next day she was released. Grandpa wheeled her out to the car. Grandma asked the doctor. "Can she still go to the Strawberry Fair on Saturday night?"

Dr. Sam Telloyan was on duty now. He was new in town, having just finished his internship at Johns Hopkins in Baltimore. He was the son of Armenian immigrants.

"Yes, she can. But don't put her on any of the rides. Violent motion like that might affect her head wound. We like this girl, but we don't want to see her around here again, understand?"

On the way home, Kosy was very serious. "Grandpa, I could have died. I was really scared."

"Kosy, where would you have gone if you had died yesterday?" Grandpa asked with great concern. "We've been praying you would understand salvation by grace through Christ."

"I'm still confused about how God loves me. Shane, can you take me to talk to Pastor Ballentine?" Now this was a change in attitude. This is what the Lynchs and the Woods families had been praying for.

That evening, Shane and Thomas took Kosy to the parsonage and rang the doorbell. Marva Ballentine answered the door. "Well, do come in. We heard about your accident yesterday, Kosy. God certainly did take care of you."

Mrs. Ballentine was a real homemaker. She was the kind of woman anyone would want for a grandmother or mother-in-law. She was kind and considerate, with all the trappings of an appreciated grandmother. "The Pastor is in the radio room talking to his brother in Brazil. You can go right in."

Pastor Ballentine heard the noise, opened the door, and motioned them to enter and take a seat. "Just a minute, and I'll sign off with my brother in Brazil. Okay, Tom, 73s and 99s old buddy, See you next week. This is WB7SQO signing off with PY3ZBA."

Shane was enthralled. "Very interesting, Pastor. Some

day I'd like to talk to your brother on the radio. Does he ever come here and preach? Actually, we are here because Kosy wants to talk to you."

"You probably know about my accident at the covered bridge yesterday," Kosy began nervously, "If ... if it hadn't been for the boy's fast action, I wouldn't be here now." With that, Kosy started to bite her fingernails, but Shane pulled her hand away from her mouth.

"Yes, I heard. What exactly do you want to talk about?"

"I want to be sure where I'll go when I die," Kosy answered. "I'm still confused about how God loves me. If He really loves me, where was He when our dads abandoned us and our mom tramped us all over the country from bar to bar?"

Pastor Ballentine had heard this desperate cry before. He knew Kosette was coming with a lot of emotional baggage, and he was not sure if he could unpack all of it in a meeting of just a few minutes. But, he was going to give it his best shot. "Christ was also abandoned by His Father when the sin of all humanity was laid on His body, Kosy. He was mistreated and voluntarily died a horrible death to pay the price of your sin and my sin. He really experienced rejection, even from those for whom He died.

"I can't answer all those questions you have. God proved His love for you when He sent His only Son to die in your place. He DOES love you and wants you to be born again. Listen to this, the most well-known verse in the Bible, John 3:16: 'For God so LOVED the world that He GAVE His only begotten Son, that whosoever believeth in Him, should not perish but have everlasting life.'

"I know you're very bitter against your mother, but you're also bitter against God. He can't be blamed for the sins of your parents against you. God never told them to do that or made them do it. They sinned against God and against you when they did those things to you. You have to be really careful, Kosy. If hatred and revenge were solid and had a form, it would be in the shape of a boomerang."

"What are you trying to say? You mean they'd eventually come back and hit me?"

"That's exactly what I'm saying. You understood perfectly. Hatred and revenge are enemies that destroy our lives. Wouldn't you like to pray tonight and ask Christ to be your personal Savior?"

Kosy looked at Shane. "What should I do?"

Shane put his hand on her shoulder. He loved his little sister with all his heart. He knew how much more she had suffered than Thomas and he had. They were there, they saw it, and it broke their hearts. They always tried to comfort her, especially when she was crying herself to sleep in a boarding home. "Now's the time, Sis. I see no reason to delay any further."

"I've got to think this thing through some more." They left the parsonage without any decision to receive Christ as Savior. Shane knew there was still much to pray about.

The trio wanted to stop at the Lynch Ranch before going home. They didn't even get to the house before a downpour hit. Mr. Lynch was holding the door open as they hurried through, soaked to their waists.

"Why don't you kids wait out the storm by playing some billiards in the family room?" Mr. Lynch suggested. "I'll park the topless Chevy in the barn, and you can thank God you have leather seats." With this, Fred grabbed the keys and headed for the drenched 'Bluebird'.

Erin grabbed Kosy and headed down the hall, answering her dad as she turned the corner. "Kosy and I have to straighten up our hair first."

While Erin was handing her brushes to Kosy, she began to talk about her most recent favorite subject. "Since Shane has accepted Christ, have you noticed any changes in his life?"

Kosy was tugging at her wet, tangled hair. "Why, yes, I have. He doesn't use bad words anymore, and every time we eat, even in a restaurant, he insists on blessing the food. Sometimes I think it's very embarrassing."

"He's doing well," Erin joyfully noted. "A real dedicated Christian is never embarrassed to claim he knows Christ. What else is new?"

"Well, he reads the Bible often and has many talks with Pastor Ballentine. He even pays attention in church. Oh yeah, can you believe this? He's even talking about giving 10% of his money to the church. And, he's always telling me he's praying for me."

These were just the kind of changes this Montana cowgirl had been praying for. Shane was on her mind all the time, but she was not going to linger on that subject if he wasn't one hundred percent sold out to the Lord and His cause. No way was she going to get interested in a mediocre Christian; there was no place in her future for a half-hearted interest in the things of God.

The girls entered the family room at the whistles of three teasing boys. "You girls look great," Shane said, "especially that transplant from The Big Sky Country." Erin blushed red but absolutely enjoyed the compliment.

They racked the balls, and Thomas broke, but all six pockets remained empty. Shane was looking out the window. "Can you believe a man is climbing up the electric pole? What in the world is he going to do up there in this rainstorm?"

"Good grief, he's putting his face up to the wire," Marty retorted. "That's dumb. There must be 40,000 volts in that line. He could be …"

There was a flash of light at the pole, dimming the room's bulbs temporarily. Thomas laid his cue stick on the table. "This guy is going to need some help. Call your parents."

When they found the victim, he was crumpled at the foot of the electric pole. Mr. Lynch turned him over and saw he was bleeding from his mouth, but breathing. "I think he broke his leg and an arm. What were you doing up there?"

"I was tryingk to lyte my cigaryette," he babbled with a slur.

It was then Mr. Lynch smelled liquor on his breath. "This poor fellow is so drunk he doesn't know what he's doing. You're lucky to be alive. I can't imagine a sane man doing what you did. You're soaking wet. Where do you live?"

The man could hardly talk as the electric jolt had knocked out his teeth. "I yive on old Simon pyace."

They put him in the car and drove him two miles to the old Simon farm. Mr. Lynch was friendly but not overly excited about these neighbors. "Your family will have to take you to a doctor right away."

As they pulled into the driveway, Shane was casing the place. What a mess! Car parts were scattered all over the yard. The uncut grass was growing up around them and through them—an old rusted-out Maytag wringer washing machine was on the front porch.

When they returned from delivering the injured man to the door, Shane asked Mr. Lynch to turn on his headlights. "Just as I thought, look at those red streaks running down the bumper of that ugly 'whatever' car in the driveway."

He got out for a closer look. He ran his hand over the back bumper. Back in the car, he examined his hand closely. "Just as I thought ... blood. These guys must be into poaching as a pastime."

As they pulled out of the narrow driveway, Erin noticed someone had opened the curtains and was watching their every move. That gave her goose bumps, and the hair stood up on the back of her neck.

11 - The Final Encounter

"This is the last night of the Strawberry Fair, Bowie," Shane pleaded on the phone. "We all want you to go with us. It'll be fun. Okay, we'll pick you up at the archery range at six o'clock. Sharpening up your aim, huh?"

Thomas was explaining the plans to Grandpa Woods. "We'll pick up the Lynches and be back before midnight. Don't worry about tomorrow. I'll be responsible for getting Kosette up and ready for church, even if I have to put an ice cube under her armpit."

Shane spent the afternoon fishing in The Channels by Snow Peak Bridge, thinking about the near tragedy that occurred there just a short time ago. It was that incident that had opened his eyes to his need for salvation. He had always believed in God, the Bible, and eternity, but had never done anything about his destiny.

He had always thought God weighed good works against sins. He now understood that type of thinking wasn't even logical! Using this method of salvation and dealing with a holy God left everyone out of heaven.

It was through Pastor Ballentine's preaching, his grandparents' changed lives, and the Lynches' witnessing that he finally came to understand salvation by grace alone, through the shed blood of Christ on the cross of Calvary. He finally settled the question of his eternal destiny by repenting of his sin and accepting Christ as his Savior.

It was a decision he had not regretted. His life was not the same since. Even his plans for the future were being molded by God. He just sat there and smiled as his bobber floated in the pool.

He had borrowed a pigeon from Mrs. Lynch and was now attaching a note to its leg. '*Irlga luspa riendfa qualsea irlfriendga, ightra*?' He turned the bird loose. "This should be a short trip. Now don't get lost, and don't stop to date or eat any worms."

Shane hurried home to pick up Thomas and Kosy. As he drove to the Lynches, he thanked God for Kosy's recovery and prayed for her salvation. "God, I want both Thomas and Kosy to know the peace that I have, knowing my sins are forgiven in Christ."

Erin ran out to the car to meet Shane. "Mom said there was a message for me on one of the pigeons. Can you imagine that? Wait right here, Shane. I need to retrieve it." His heart was pounding so loud he thought Thomas and Kosy could hear it.

When Erin rounded the corner of the barn, she was smiling so big she almost broke her face. She was also blushing a little. "Shane, no wonder my mother couldn't understand the note. How sweet of you. So you speak three languages: English, Spanish, and Pig Latin. Wow, you're really talented!"

Irlga luspa riendfa qualsea irlfriendga, ightra?

Translated from Pig Latin to English:
'Girl plus friend equals girlfriend, right?'

Erin was patting Shane's hand on the car door when Marty came out. "Hey, what's this, two more members in the teenage mutual admiration society? Let's get going before all the strawberry shortcake is gone."

At the archery range, Bowie was putting his last arrow in the bull's-eye. Shane was impressed. "Nine out of ten in the bulls-eye area. Not bad for a gas station worker! Where did you learn to shoot like that? Can you teach me?"

"My Uncle Elk Looks Back gave me lessons. He's a great police officer in Pendleton, over in Eastern Oregon. I've had a lot of practice. It's something I like to do. Let's put the stuff in the trunk and go straight to the fair."

When they turned onto Tangent Street, they found a parking space right by the main gate. Shane backed up, parking parallel on the first try, but he scraped the tires on the curb.

"Not bad for a California driver," Bowie teased, getting his revenge.

The fairgrounds were crowded. Shane could see the clowns at the far end, up to their usual pranks. He pointed them out to Bowie. "Those guys are obnoxious. Last time we were here, they really roughed me up. Maybe they don't like us, because we seem to be the only ones they get rough with."

First came the strawberry shortcake, since the line wasn't very long. Thomas was finishing his third bowl when he commented to Marty. "We'd better let this settle a bit before we get on any of those gut-twisting, brain-bashing rides."

They made the rounds to see all the exhibits, including the two-headed calf and the rubber man. Bowie looked interested. "If I could do those bends and curves like the rubber man, I'd never be beaten as a wrestler. Do you think he would give lessons?"

The clowns came flying by again, and this time they plowed into the boys, knocking them flat. Then, they ran on laughing. Shane was helping Marty up. "Those guys ought to be fired. They're not clowns, they're jerks."

The rock-o-plane was the first mind-bender they tried. Shane forgot to take his change out of his pockets again. He didn't even think about it until he heard it clatter to the ceiling when they were upside down.

Kosy could only watch with envy as the gang boarded the octopus. Erin looked sympathetic. "Sorry, Kosy, doctor's orders. We want you to get completely healed." Thomas was even more firm than that, giving a few orders that just made Kosy shake her head at him.

Kosy let out a session of protests, but it was for naught, with someone as stubborn as Thomas. She sat in the grass and pouted. "I guess I'll just have to wait until next year."

"THE OCTOPUS"
CIRCUS RIDE
(CA 1963)

Now came the brain scrambler. Shane and Erin were right behind Thomas and Bowie. Marty had to ride with a girl he didn't know. Just as they got airborne and began twirling like a top, the clowns descended on Kosy, turning her upside down and shaking her around.

Thomas was indignant, but all he could do was yell. "Hey, you clowns, leave my sister alone. She has a head injury. Just wait until I get down from here."

Shane and Erin began yelling at the clowns, too. By the time the octopus stopped, Kosy was picking grass out of her hair. She was visibly shaken and stuttering. "Those g ... guys are nuts. I'm going to complain to the fair officials."

"But, Kosy, remember they don't work for the fair company," Erin made a point of it.

Shane scratched his head. "Then they must work for the Strawberry Fair committee."

With the hours passing, they decided to head for Lacomb. As they approached the car, Erin noticed it first. "Someone around here doesn't like us, Shane."

Written with pink spray paint all down the side of the car were the famous words: "KILROY WAS HERE."

"Who's Kilroy?" Kosy asked.

"I'll explain that later," Shane promised as he noticed Mark Poorman coming towards them. Mr. Poorman had been Shane's sixth-grade teacher at the junior high across the street.

"Good evening, Mr. Poorman," Shane said, extending a warm, friendly hand. "Aren't you on the Strawberry Fair Committee?"

Mr. Poorman was dumbfounded. "Well, look at this. The Woods kids have invaded Lebanon again. Are you living around here now? To answer your question, yes, I'm on the committee."

"Well, those clowns you hired to spread joy and happiness among the good citizens of Linn County aren't doing anything but causing havoc and disrupting the troops. They almost gave my sister, Kosy, a headache by bouncing her upside down. This is a bit too much, don't you think?"

Mr. Poorman looked puzzled. "I'm not sure what you're talking about, Shane. We didn't hire any clowns. I thought those men were rude, too. The Strawberry fair personnel office must've hired them."

Now Shane was really concerned, "Do you know for sure the committee didn't hire those dumb clowns?"

"Absolutely, Shane," Mr. Poorman looked bewildered now. "I'm the chairman of the committee. No doubt about it."

"Then there's something rotten in Denmark and it ain't the pigs." Shane looked at the rest of the crew. "If they don't work for the committee or for the fair company, then they must be on their own." Shane began to put the jigsaw puzzle together.

"Why don't they like us?" With that on his mind, the young Sherlock began stroking his chin. "Wait a minute, wait just a cotton-picking minute. The Snow Peak robbers were here last time we were roughed up, right?"

Erin started thinking, too. "Remember, those three crooks that chased us. Each one put a big duffel bag in the trunk. Those could've been their clown clothes."

"They must be using the clown outfits as a diversion," Marty concluded. "They're up to no good. Everywhere they go, mischief and pain follow behind like the tail of a tornado."

Shane moved quickly now. "Mr. Poorman, if you can get to a phone, would you please contact Sergeant

Kochian or anyone at the police station and tell them the Snow Peak robbers are going to assault the fair ticket office?"

"Are you sure, Shane. That's a lot of guessing, don't you think?"

"Putting all the loose ends together, that's the most logical conclusion I can come up with," Shane answered with as much confidence as he could muster. "They're apparently using the clown outfits for cover."

"Fine, then. I'll phone from my office in the junior high."

As Mr. Poorman ran to the junior high building, Shane had another idea. "Let's go warn the ticket office. Maybe we can prevent a robbery."

As they approached the office, they noticed the door ajar. Bowie looked in. "They've already been here. The unlucky cashier is out cold."

"Look, Thomas," Kosy exclaimed, pulling on his shirt. "They're just running out the front gate." In hot

pursuit, the group passed the main gate just in time to see the clowns enter the far parking lot and get into a car no one could recognize.

Thomas was determined. "They're not going to get away this time. Shane, you do the driving. Marty, tell the gate guard what's happened and ask him to send Sergeant Kochian west on Tangent Street. Bowie, get your bow from the trunk."

While Thomas was barking orders like a sergeant, the clowns fishtailed onto Tangent Street, heading west, just as Thomas had predicted. Loaded with anxious and angry teens, the '51 Chevy followed after them. The crooks now had a car so ugly not even Shane could tell what it was.

"It's probably stolen, and no one would really miss a car that ugly." Shane surmised.

The '51 Chevy was building speed after crossing the railroad tracks. The top velocity for this old, worn-out eggbeater was about sixty-five miles per hour, if the hamster in the flywheel was in good shape. It was all-or-nothing for the six nervous riders.

"They took a left on 9th Street," Thomas noted.

When Shane slowed way down to make a sharp left turn, the passenger door flew open. Marty had been leaning hard on it. Clinging to the door, he flew out of his seat, holding all his weight up with his right arm over the window.

"Hold on, Marty. Keep your feet up," Erin yelled. "Shane, make a right turn."

Fortunately, the crooks turned right on Isabella Street. When the blue Chevy made a sharp turn to the right, Marty came scooting back in his place. When the door shut hard, Bowie locked it.

Marty was still dumbfounded about how he had exited and entered so smoothly. He was getting a nervous bounce in his right leg. "We want to follow these guys, but we don't want an accident."

The burned-out, ugly, blue car turned back towards Tangent Street. Realizing they were being followed, the crooks headed for the open highway. By the time Shane got onto Tangent, he could see police cars just turning the corner at the junior high. Their red lights were blazing. Thomas handed Bowie an arrow for his bow. "Do you think you can hit that back tire?"

"I'll try," Bowie said as he stood up. He braced his right foot in the crease of the back seat and his left knee on the top of the front seat. Just as he let fly an arrow with a hunting tip, the car hit a hole. He missed. "Can you get any closer, Shane?"

"This old baby is screaming now, but I'll put my foot in the carburetor." Shane gained a little on the unknown car, and Bowie released another missile. POW, right on the mark. The rusted-out bucket of bolts began to swerve. It rolled on its side, then came back up on its wheels, broadsiding a telephone pole. The old car doubled in the middle as the driver's door slammed into the pole.

"Ram it, Shane," Thomas ordered. "Crush the other door or they'll escape again."

"But my car!" This was the only thing he owned.

"Forget the car. We can get another one."

"Everyone, brace yourself." Shane slowed down to about twenty miles per hour and torpedoed the '51 Chevy into the thug's passenger door, trapping the three crooks inside, making the ultra-ugly car uglier (if that was even possible)!

The teenagers jumped over the side like rats abandoning a sinking ship. They took off for the high country, just in case the crooks decided to take some pot shots out the windows.

Sergeant Kochian arrived just as the dust was settling and 'Bluebird's' radiator was leaking. The three unhappy criminals were unceremoniously dragged from between the two wrecked cars and arrested. The boss was beside himself. He managed to yell through all his ugly, smeared makeup. "I'll get you kids for this."

"Shane, here you are again mixed up in the action," Sergeant Kochian marveled. "Are you lucky or what?"

"Either I'm always in the wrong place at the right time or the right place at the wrong time," Shane babbled.

"What was that you said?" Kosy looked perplexed.

"Look at my car. Totaled out. It wasn't much, but it was all I had," Shane complained as he let out a deep sigh. The 'Bluebird' had flown south for the winter. Permanently!

Kosy felt like a good friend had just died. The '51 Chevy had been their only continuity until they arrived at Grandpa's farm. The blue convertible had transferred them to happier times and had served as an ambulance when Kosy's life needed saving. Tears clouded her blue, luminous eyes, and her lips began to tremble.

"Look at poor 'Bluebird', Shane. She's crying, too." Kosy was pointing to the leaking radiator.

Shane felt as bad as Kosy did, but he was trying to live up to his macho image. He shook his head several times to clear it. It seemed there were tears in his own eyes, too.

"Listen, Shane," Sergeant Kochian said, "We're so happy to finally capture Horace Power and his robbing murderers. You sacrificed all you had to make sure they didn't escape. I think there's something down at the city pound that might interest you. Can you come back tomorrow afternoon? We'll have an official decision by then."

On the way home, Kosy reminded Shane to explain what 'KILROY WAS HERE' meant. Shane took the teacher's position.

"Kilroy was working in a WW II ammunition supply depot. His boss thought he was goofing off. So to prove he wasn't, he wrote KILROY (his name) WAS HERE on every 10th box of supplies going to the troops. When the troops got the boxes, they began to speculate who he was. They finally found out. Now, anyone who wants to say 'I have been here, take notice' writes KILROY WAS HERE."

Officer Quinten Freeburg drove the six tired teens home. The next day, Bowie joined them. Mr. Lynch was at the city impound lot to take pictures for the Lebanon Express. Shane was grinning like a Cheshire cat.

"This 1957 Chevrolet convertible was confiscated last month from Fora DaLei. She's a criminal who won't need it where she is going," Sergeant Kochian announced proudly. "It has four special features: the transmission has been changed to a four-on-the-floor, the motor has been bored out 60 cc's over normal, it has a four-barreled carburetor, and, for some weird reason, no one here can explain, the front window can fold down flat."

"It's all yours, Shane, lock, stock, and four barrels," Officer Freeburg added. "The title will be transferred to your grandfather's name, but it's your car. All of us here at the office pitched in to prepay one year of insurance."

"Now," Mr. Lynch requested, "all six of you get next to the '57 Chevy for a picture, but don't hide the nice car."

Officer Freeburg asked, "Just for the record, Shane, is that your girlfriend standing next to you?"

Shane put his arm around Erin's shoulder. "She's already been a girl and a friend. Is she my girlfriend, you want to know?" Shane glanced at Erin with a mischievous look in his eyes. "Well, I think that might depend on whether she's applying for the job."

Erin didn't know precisely how to interpret Shane's strange look and comments, so she just smiled warmly for the cameraman.

TO BE CONTINUED

The 1957 Chevy Bel Air convertible is considered one of the all-time classic cars, like a Corvette or a Thunderbird. Its dynamic style has made it more desirable and valuable today.

Shane Woods Series

Book One: *The Snow Peak Robbers*
            ISBN 978-1-885708-51-9

Book Two: *The Strawberry Fair*
            ISBN 978-1-885708-52-6

Book Three: *The Buzzard Butte Poachers*
            ISBN 978-1-885708-53-3

Book Four: *The Eastern Rodeo*
            ISBN 978-1-885708-54-0

Future books will depend on reader interest. More book sales may motivate me to publish more of my existing manuscripts.

The Nez Perce Tribe

www.nezperce.org

Ollokot, Chief Joseph, and Peo-Peo-Tah-Likt
Colorized photo from the National Park Service
Nez Perce Historical Images Collection

The Nez Perce Tribe is a federally recognized tribe in North Central Idaho with more than 3,500 enrolled citizens. Headquartered in Lapwai, ID, the Nez Perce Reservation spans about 770,000 acres.

The current governmental structure is based on a constitution adopted by the tribe in 1948. The tribe is governed by a nine-member elected executive committee, known as the Nez Perce Tribal Executive Committee (NPTEC). The NPTEC is obligated to protect the health and welfare of the Nez Perce people. This means protecting and preserving treaty rights and tribal sovereignty, Nez Perce culture, and the reservation's general environment.

History

The Nimiipuu people have been connected to the lands and waters of modern-day Idaho, Washington, Oregon, and Montana long before the creation of the Nez Perce Reservation.

Culture

Today, the Nez Perce Tribe upholds many traditional lifeways, including fishing, hunting, gathering, and traditional ceremonies and celebrations.

Language

The Nimipuutímt language is an integral part of Nez Perce culture. Their language program offers learning tools to keep the language thriving.

Author Biography

Dr. Tom Latham

Tom Latham became a Christian while serving in the U.S. Navy, where he began holding *Protestant Divine Services* whenever his ship was at sea. After

completing his naval service, he spent the next four years at Bible College to further his spiritual journey. He achieved a significant milestone in his studies by earning a Doctor of Ministry (DMin) degree from Luther Rice Seminary.

Tom met Penny Stimpson, and together they began
a mission to serve God in Brazil. Their family grew
to include three children, six grandchildren, and ten
great-grandchildren.

Although Penny was promoted to Glory, Tom continues
to serve Christ in Brazil.

*To read more details about Dr. Latham's educational
journey, visit www.brazilwrestler.com.*

Acknowledgments

I want to acknowledge Jesus Christ, my Savior. Without His guidance and grace lifting me from a worldly ditch, this book would not exist. I owe Him more than I can ever repay.

I want to thank my three children, Thomas, Shane, and Kosette, for making life an adventure as we faced the challenges and joys of the mission field in Brazil. Their companionship gave us more experiences than those in my more than 70 manuscripts, which may soon become published books.

I also want to thank Dave Carlson for his invaluable contribution to the publishing process. His tremendous efforts far exceeded what I could have accomplished alone, and I am deeply grateful.

www.ingramcontent.com/pod-product-compliance
Lightning Source LLC
Chambersburg PA
CBHW050030040726
47599CB00015B/1608